HOW TO WRITE ABOUT MUSIC

THE RILM MANUAL OF STYLE

Second Edition

James R. Cowdery, editor

Foreword by Carl A. Skoggard
Introduction by Barbara Dobbs Mackenzie

RÉPERTOIRE INTERNATIONAL DE LITTÉRATURE MUSICALE, NEW YORK

THE RÉPERTOIRE INTERNATIONAL DE LITTÉRATURE MUSICALE was founded in 1966. It is sponsored by the International Musicological Society and the International Association of Music Libraries, Archives, and Documentation Centres and is governed by a Commission Internationale Mixte designated by the sponsors. The operation of the International Center is made possible through the kind cooperation of The Graduate Center of the City University of New York. RILM publications include *RILM abstracts of music literature*, a continuously updated, international guide to writings on music, available in print, on CD-ROM, and online.

COMMISSION INTERNATIONALE MIXTE: Veslemöy Heintz, president; Chris Banks, vice president; H. Robert Cohen, Suzanne G. Cusick, David Fallows, Massimo Gentili-Tedeschi, Wolfgang Kreuger, Martie Severt, Philippe Vendrix, Chris Walton.

Barbara Dobbs Mackenzie, *Editor-in-Chief*
Zdravko Blažeković, *Executive Editor*

Répertoire Internationale de Littérature Musicale

365 Fifth Avenue
New York, NY 10016
www.rilm.org

Printed in the United States of America.
12 11 10 09 08 07 06   1 2 3 4 5

ISBN-10: 1-932765-03-4
ISBN-13: 978-1-932765-03-8

Cover: *St. Gregory with the scribes* (Carolingian, late 9th century). Ivory, 20.5 × 12.5 cm. Vienna, Kunsthistorisches Museum, inv. no. 8399. Reproduced with permission.

Layout and design by J. Graeme Fullerton.
Cover design by fredgatesdesign.com.
Printing by Port City Press, Baltimore, MD.

This book is printed on acid-free paper.

TABLE OF CONTENTS

FOREWORD

For many years, our organization did without any written manual of style. Dorothy Curzon, the office boss back then, served as oral authority of last resort. She had copyedited for *The New Yorker* under William Shawn and knew her commas. The path to her desk was a well-worn one, and I myself learned much from her patient replies. Alas for her, many of the same elementary queries would come up time and again: Unformed minds tend to think alike and to ask the same simple questions. "Commas always come in pairs" might do very nicely as part of an unveiling of the mystery of the unrestrictive clause, but you had to want to know, and she had to be prepared to repeat this lesson for each new petitioner. Then, too, with more recondite issues, Dorothy could turn oracular. "That depends" or "It's a matter of taste, you know" left one with a regard for the mysteries of our guild though not necessarily any wiser. (There are in fact mysteries for which the most detailed manual cannot account, but not many.)

In the early days, RILM processed only a fraction of what it must contend with today. Dorothy managed to go over everything before it went to press, grooming away what was still bearish in her sous-editors' copy. But for some two decades now, RILM has depended on various incarnations of a house style manual. The advent of a manual—the codification of explicit editing rules—was imperative if we were to cope with the growing challenge of coverage, let alone thrive. Successive RILM house style manuals reflect every stage of our recent evolution, which has been driven by continual advances in information technology. Every RILM chieftain since Dorothy has left a version of the manual behind. (These make for amusing reading for anyone who lived through the crises of whichever moment it happened to be in the history of RILM.) The present compendium, however, is more than our latest house manual dressed up for an outing. *How to write about music* is intended to meet the needs of anyone who wants to write conscientiously about music. In a spirit opposed to guild exclusivity, we are determined to share with you the benefits of RILM's experience with virtually every kind of writing about music, from all over the world, for 40 years.

Readers will see that this guide proceeds, roughly, from the general to the specialized. Some of what is offered applies to academic writing as a whole, but most concerns the very particular craft of writing effectively and well about the art we all love above the rest. *How to write about music* reflects RILM's daily encounters with not only Western materials, but also with writings from Japan, India, China—from everywhere, in fact, where people are busy producing studies of music. It applies an international perspective to matters usually dealt with in piecemeal and ethnocentric fashion: transliteration, city names, institutional names, work titles. *How to write about music* deals with popular musics as well as art traditions. Liturgists, librarians, critics, performers, postmodernists, and premodernists will find answers to their questions. Throughout, abundant examples illustrate each point. There are detailed and sophisticated guidelines for the bibliographic handling of online and other non-print material. There are even guidelines for how to write a good abstract and submit it to RILM.

Since the undersigned had nothing to do with its preparation, he feels free to say that the virtues of *How to write about music* include, but are not limited to, succinctness, comprehensiveness, and a refreshing absence of dogmatism. Certainly this is the most ambitious guide of its kind. Some could fear that such a rulebook must encroach on the writer's preserve, leaving him or her feeling over-regulated and under-authorial. It is not the case, however. Persuasion—an appeal to the writer's good common sense—always remains the aim, not prescription.

Anonymous RILM (fl. 1971–2005)

PREFACE TO THE SECOND EDITION

When we published the first edition of *How to write about music: The RILM manual of style* in 2005, we assumed that a revised second edition would be in order at some point. Although the original book represented many years of experience and thought, we suspected that we would identify other matters that should be covered, and we anticipated—and invited—suggestions from readers. This new edition, which is roughly one-third larger than the first, includes responses to suggestions, revisions, and new material.

The largest single addition is a chapter on indexing. Since authors of monographs often must compile their own indexes, and since RILM has 40 years of experience in indexing writings about music, it seemed natural for us to offer assistance. The new chapter explains how we approach indexing, and provides suggestions for adapting our system for individual indexing projects.

Also, we decided to make a general revision to chapter 16, *Citations*. As Barbara Dobbs Mackenzie explained in her introduction to the first edition, the bibliographic formats in that chapter were based on those in *The Chicago manual of style* rather than on the formats used in RILM's printed volumes. We later realized that RILM's formats, which were perfected over the course of three decades, were no less worthy than those of other publishers—in fact, they are easier to use, since the same bibliographic information is always handled in the same way. A publisher will convert citations to its own house style regardless of how an author formats them, so why not offer our simple, clear system as an alternative for those preparing manuscripts or writing papers? Accordingly, RILM standards are now available here and through online bibliographic management services.

Other additions include formats for citing reference publications, tertiary sources (including *Grove* and *MGG*), reviews, correspondence, manuscripts, and notes and commentary in scores and editions. A section on transliterating Chinese languages has been added, and small revisions have been made throughout the book. Although we do not plan to issue a third edition in the near future, we will always be grateful for suggestions for further improvements.

JRC

INTRODUCTION

How to write about music: The RILM manual of style lays out policies and procedures for issues that confront every author of texts about music. We have aimed to state each point clearly and concisely, with illustrative examples that pertain primarily to the realm of music. The first and second chapters deal with certain general elements of writing style that are commonly questioned, such as how best to achieve gender-neutral prose, the difference between an en dash and an em dash, and other nagging matters of punctuation. Should *choirbook* have a hyphen? What about *ear training*, or *fieldwork*, for that matter? Is it really *pre-Classical* but *postimpressionism*? Where do the hyphens properly go in *four three-to-ten-year-old children*? Is it *Brahms'* or *Brahms's*?

Next come chapters 3 through 9, treating issues frequently encountered by writers on music, though not specifically musical in nature. How does one handle plurals in non-English words? Is it *libretti* or *librettos*, and how should the plurals of *concerto grosso* and *opera buffa* be formed? Common misspellings are cleared up (*a cappella*, in RILM office lore, is the single most commonly misspelled term in academic texts, often bereft of a *p*). Are conference names rendered in italics or roman? There is no space in K.440, nor in d.1970, but when the city of Jimi Hendrix's death is included, a space is needed (d. London 1970). Should you write mridangam, *mridangam*, or mṛdaṅgam? When is trecento capitalized and when isn't it? Even the mysteries of alphabetizing Pedro Calderón de la Barca, Mairéad Ní Mhaonaigh, and 'Abd al-Qāder al-Marāghī are revealed.

Chapters 10 through 14 tackle musical problems. When should one use quotation marks and when italics for work titles? Under what circumstances may translations and common nicknames be used? Why is it *Missa "L'homme armé"* but *Missa La sol fa re mi*? How and when should one include opus and catalogue numbers? How are manuscripts cited and how do those encrypted RISM sigla work? Conquer the complexities of pitch, chord, scale, and mode designations, both Western and non-Western, as well as the construction of captions for in-text musical examples.

RILM could not publish a manual without chapters on abstract writing (15), bibliographic citation (16), and indexing (17)—procedures upon which our reputation has rested for 40 years. Authors of dissertations and theses traditionally write abstracts of their tomes; but increasingly, journal publishers are requesting such summaries from their authors as well. Then there is the practice—ingrained in well-behaved scholars—of submitting abstracts of all their publications to *RILM abstracts of music literature*.

And yet, in many quarters, the fine art of writing a good abstract has remained dark and mysterious. Until now.

Chapter 16, significantly expanded and somewhat changed in this second edition of our manual, provides citation formats for footnotes, endnotes, and bibliographies. No existing bibliographic style authority covers many of the specialized sources relied upon by contemporary writers on music. Thus Chapter 16 provides citation formats for online and other e-publications, liner notes, program notes, technical drawings of instruments, scores, sound recordings, videos, radio broadcasts, and more.

The final chapter, newly added in this edition, provides a how-to guide on indexing, a procedure few writers on music have any experience with before confronting the task. Here you will find suggestions for getting started and for organizing and arranging the concepts, names, and places addressed in your prose in a logical, clear, and useful manner following some of the RILM principles for indexing.

The policies contained herein reflect RILM's mission and will not coincide with every reader's common practice. As an international, collaborative project to abstract and index writings about music, RILM strives for global coverage, and our house style aims to serve this breadth of material as accurately and even-handedly as possible. We adopt international standards whenever it is possible to do so, avoiding standards peculiar to any one country. One example of this is RILM's transliteration systems for non-roman alphabets: RILM follows those published by the International Organization for Standarization (ISO), not the National Information Standards Organization (NISO) of the U.S. or any other country-specific system. Therefore, RILM spells that well-known 19th-century Russian composer Čajkovskij, consciously eschewing Tchaikovsky, with the full knowledge that in certain English-speaking countries the latter is widely used. (For a fuller discussion of this policy, see page 58.) An international perspective—inclusive of all the world's cultures and writings—is at the very heart of RILM.

We have worked to organize the manual and its index to allow for quick dips in and out as specific questions arise. But consider, as well, diving in headlong and freestyling from one end to the other. You may find the waters surprisingly invigorating. No doubt you will come upon many topics for which you need no refresher or instruction; but there will almost certainly be other sections that illuminate submerged pockets of uncertainty in your mind.

Countless RILM editors have contributed to our manual, and all deserve to be named, as their opinions, ideas, and sometimes even their prose are found here in one form or another. It would be impossible to account individually for each one's contributions, so we must content ourselves instead with tipping our hat collectively to all those who have had a hand in forming the RILM style over the years. Two individuals, however, deserve special mention: E. Terence Ford wrote the first substantial style manual for RILM when he was an editor in the mid-1980s; he continued to refine it during his tenure as Editor-in-Chief (1988–91). Adam P.J. O'Connor succeeded Terry in that position, and he amplified the document significantly in his own distinctive voice until his untimely death in 1996. These two each left behind a fine version of the manual, and we continue to be indebted to their efforts, expertise, and prose.

Because so many have contributed to the manual, the reader may notice the changing timbre of multiple voices. We have retained, to a certain degree, these variations and nuances of tone, not only because we at RILM enjoy encountering the voices of our old colleagues herein, but because they mirror the collaborative, democratic, and inclusive nature of RILM, a nature we hold dear. We hope that some of this is transmitted through these pages, enlivening them with hints of RILM's past and present culture—of the lengthy discussions common, no doubt, to all editorial offices; of echoes of past and current personalities and sensibilities; and, especially, of the daily inspiration of working with the world's stunningly rich musical scholarship.

Is our manual exhaustive? No. *The RILM manual of style* is an organic entity, a never-ending work in progress. It will continue to grow and change over time as the disciplines and modes of music and its study change. The manual will grow, too, simply because—even after years of tinkering—we still come across new problems to solve. We continue to encourage readers to alert us to areas you would like us to address, or address more fully; we will carefully collect such suggestions and ideas for future editions. Collaboration is at the core of the RILM enterprise, and has been from the day Barry S. Brook founded it. We invite you to join the ranks and become a RILM collaborator yourself.

Barbara Dobbs Mackenzie, Editor-in-Chief

1. STYLE

1.1 Choosing a title

Titles should point to topics; they need not entertain. In print, a mysterious or clever title may stimulate interest, but in an electronic world it can have the opposite effect: People searching in electronic databases may never find the item, even if it is directly relevant to their concerns. If you want your work to be discovered, be sure that your title includes the keywords that will lead interested readers to it.

1.2 Dead language

Avoid obfuscation, periphrasis, pretensions, and other kinds of dead language.

> affects, **not** impacts on
>
> use, **not** utilize
>
> uses, **not** makes use of

Say it in one word, not three (or more):

> during Lent, **not** between the beginning of Lent and Easter
>
> variation involves, **not** variation is a technique that involves
>
> symphonies and concertos, **not** on the one hand, symphonies, and, on the other, concertos

Refrain from needless repetition, modification, and self-praise:

> limits, **not** limits and constraints
>
> an analysis, **not** a complete analysis
>
> examination reveals, **not** a careful examination reveals

Eschew twisty passive constructions and meandering prepositional phrases:

> male troupes entertain at festivals, **not** men are organized together in troupes that provide entertainment at festivals
>
> began collecting songs in 1887, **not** first began the activity of the collection of songs in the year 1887

Not only . . . but also is not only overused, but also rarely necessary. Use it only when it is needed to distinguish between opposing views; otherwise, change it to *both*.

> She is known as both a performer and a scholar.

And/or is inelegant, and should be avoided; in most cases it may be replaced by *or*.

> They provide grants to young or little-known composers.

Do not use an unassimilated foreign term when an English one exists:

> reception history, **not** *Rezeptionsgeschichte*

1.3 Gender issues

1.3.1 Neutral language

The most common issue in this area is the pronoun problem: how to avoid using *he* when speaking generally. The solution of using *they* or *their* when the antecedent is singular, although there are literary precedents for it going back centuries, is to be avoided because it sets some people's teeth on edge. It is better to recast the entire sentence in the plural:

> As he advances in his program, the student has increasing opportunities for ensemble work.
>
> **becomes**
>
> As they advance in their program, students have increasing opportunities for ensemble work.

Another solution is to change the sentence to avoid using any pronoun:

> A first grader can feed and dress himself.
>
> **becomes**
>
> A first grader can eat and get dressed without assistance.

He or she, *he/she*, and their inversions are tiresome; they should be avoided.

Repudiate unnecessarily gendered terms: prefer *people* to *mankind*, and so on.

1.3.2 *Female* vs. *women*

Use *women* as a descriptive noun instead of *female* whenever possible: *women's studies, women composers, all-women ensemble*. In certain cases *female* is more appropriate (e.g., *female impersonator*, or if the discussion includes young girls).

1.3.3 Sexual orientation terminology

Terms widely used in various academic contexts may or may not be the best ones for particular topics. While *heterosexual, homosexual*, and *transgender* are clinical and distancing, they must sometimes be preferred to terms like *straight, gay, lesbian, queer*, or *drag*. In other cases, terms in the latter group are more appropriate. Here are some guidelines:

Gay usually indicates both a sexual orientation and a cultural identity. It is most commonly applied to men, but it is sometimes used as a shorthand for both male and female same-sex relations. Because of its implied cultural component, caution must be taken in applying it—particularly when writing about historical figures. *Lesbian* is applied only to female same-sex relations.

Queer and *drag* are used in discourse associated with the academic field of queer studies. Within that domain, the terms are widely used and have well-defined meanings; otherwise they should be avoided due to their potentially pejorative connotations.

When in doubt, err on the side of the more clinical terms.

In references to sexual aspects of the works of persons who may or may not be gay or lesbian, the words *homoerotic* and *homoeroticism* may prove useful: They shift the focus from the person to the work.

1.4 Interpolations

Writing is most effective when it flows uninterrupted. However, there are times when interpolations are called for; these include the need to cite sources (see *16: Citations*) and qualifiers and examples that may be set in parentheses (see *2.12: Parentheses and brackets*). Interpolations comprising more than one or two brief sentences are probably best put in notes or, for electronic publications, in hyperlinks.

1.4.1 Substantive notes and hyperlinks

Whenever possible, put note numbers at the end of a sentence. Substantive end- or footnotes may include citations, or they may not:

[1] Notable 18th-century British ballad sources include D'Urfey's *Wit and mirth, or, Pills to purge melancholy* (1719–20), Ramsay's *The tea-table miscellany* (1724–27), Thomson's *Orpheus caledonius* (1725, 1733), Percy's *Reliques of ancient English poetry* (1765), and Herd's *Ancient and modern Scottish songs: Heroic ballads* (1769, 1776).

[2] Even today, printed sources for ballads are not always reliable. Unless they are clearly the work of trained folklorists or ethnomusicologists, they must be treated more as templates of performances than as transcriptions of them.

For the first example, full citations would be provided in the bibliography (see *16: Citations*).

Hyperlinks in electronic publications may lead to brief interpolations such as those above, to citations (see *16: Citations*), to illustrations (see *14: Illustrations*), to longer passages that would usually be deemed too extensive for footnotes, to sound or video files, or, for online publications, to outside resources.

2. PUNCTUATION

2.1 Spacing

Use one space after commas, semicolons, colons, and periods, including periods in ellipses (see *13.3: Introducing changes*). Do not put spaces between initials:

> Contrary to the claims of orthodox Schenkerians, Neumeyer drew heavily on the writings of Schenker's most prolific student, F.E. von Cube. The controversy surrounding Neumeyer's work . . .

Do not put spaces around dashes, hyphens, or slashes.

See also *3.3: Punctuating abbreviations*.

2.1.1 Compound words and words with prefixes and suffixes

Most standard American dictionaries have lists of words under *anti*, *counter*, *non*, *post*, *pre*, *over*, *re*, *un*, *under*, etc., Here are some compounds that come up in writings about music:

avant-garde	offbeat
cofounder	onscreen
choirbook	onstage (adj.)
cross-cultural	part song
data bank	part-time (adj.)
database	pitch class
ear training	postimpressionism
fieldwork	roundtable (discussion)
folk song	set class
folklife	set-class analysis
folklore	sight reader
folktale	songbook
lifelong	songwriter
neoclassical	sound field
nonmusical	soundscape

Prefixes are generally unhyphenated. Exceptions usually involve a repeated letter:

de-emphasize   post-tonal
non-notated   semi-independent

If the modified word is capitalized, hyphenate, preserving the capital:

anti-Semitism   pre-Classic
non-Western

Favor hyphenating terms over using an *o* to join two words:

music-historical, **not** musicohistorical

harmonic-contrapuntal, **not** harmonicocontrapuntal

However, some compounds formed with an *o* are widely accepted:

the field of sociolinguistics

a socioeconomic study

When a noun is combined with a past or present participle, the adjectival compound is hyphenated:

problem-solving skills

government-sponsored events

Some noun and participle pairs are always one word:

a bookkeeping program

When a noun is combined with a gerund (which looks just like a present participle but functions as a noun), a hyphen is not used:

music making at home

skillful piano playing

See also *2.6: The hyphen.*

2.2 The comma

See also *5.2.2: Large numbers*; *5.4: Page ranges*; *10.3: Opus and catalogue numbers.*

2.2.1 Appositives

Use commas in pairs to set off parenthetical remarks or appositive words or phrases:

> The composer Easley Blackwood, who works with microtones, was . . .

If the appositive restricts, it is not set off by commas:

> The composer Easley Blackwood

> **but**

> The oldest composer in the group, Easley Blackwood, was . . .

Some other examples:

> His favorite opera, *Lohengrin*, opened in Paris the next day.

> Wagner's opera *Lohengrin* opened in Paris the next day.

> Jay Ungar, a fiddler, was featured.

> The fiddler Jay Ungar was featured.

2.2.2 Place names

Use commas to set off the individual elements in names of places:

> They stopped in Ashtabula, Ohio, that evening.

2.2.3 The serial comma

The serial comma appears between items in a list *and* before the conjunction. It is standard in some (but not all) U.S. style manuals, and instances arise where it aids intelligibility:

> Her family was renowned for its composers, pedagogues, and violin makers and players.

Do not insert the serial comma when citing titles or quoting passages where it is not used; in British English and in many European languages the serial comma is considered wrong.

2.2.4 With *Jr.*, *III*, etc.

Do not use commas with these in prose:

> Berry Gordy Jr. founded Motown Records in 1959.

2.3 The semicolon

Do not capitalize the beginning of a full sentence following a semicolon.

2.3.1 Independent clauses

Use a semicolon to join two clauses only when each could stand on its own as a sentence:

> She severely criticizes Beethoven; his music strikes her as patriarchal and violent.

2.3.2 Serial semicolons

Use a semicolon to separate items in a list when the items themselves contain commas. A semicolon should appear before the conjunction:

> Most of his manuscripts are in the Bodleian Library; the Wilson Collection, Yale University; the Biblioteca Apostolica Vaticana; and Butler Library, Columbia University.

When items are especially long or complex, it is permissible to separate them with semicolons and enumerate them with arabic numbers in parentheses (see *5.2.1: Numbering series in sentences*).

2.3.3 Bibliographic data

Elements of equal significance in bibliographic data are separated with semicolons. See also *5.4: Page ranges*; *16.2.1: City names*.

2.4 The colon

In prose, the colon may be used only after the equivalent of a complete sentence; it should not be preceded by words like *include*, *contain*, and *are*.

Capitalize after a colon if what follows is a complete sentence:

> Keep the tempo steady: Do not use rubato.

Do not capitalize after a colon if what follows is a list or a sentence fragment:

> Danckert disputed Vicentino's views about three tetrachord genera: diatonic, chromatic, and enharmonic.

Always capitalize after a colon in a title:

> *Christus: A mystery*

2.5 The period

See *2.11.3: End punctuation with quotation marks*; *3.3: Punctuating abbreviations*.

2.6 The hyphen

Hyphenate multiword substantives thus:

> 17th-century opera
>
> the as yet half-finished auditorium
>
> six five-year-old children
>
> four three-to-ten-year-old children
>
> four-to-seven-year-olds
>
> first-grade students (**but** first graders)
>
> 9th- and 10th-century monastic libraries
>
> the mid-15th century
>
> mid–15th-century church tradition (see *2.7: The en dash*)

Some compounds are integral and never require internal hyphenation to signal that they are being used adjectivally:

> high school students
>
> South American culture
>
> World War II industry

A numbered century has no hyphen unless it is being used as an adjective:

> 18th-century keyboard works
>
> keyboard works from the 18th century

Similarly:

> Nadine's grande-dame attitude seemed unwarranted.
>
> Lady Prunella fancied herself a grande dame.

Do not hyphenate after adverbs ending in -*ly*:

> physically challenged persons, **not** physically-challenged persons

Do hyphenate if ambiguity is likely:

> late-blooming ingenue, **not** late blooming ingenue

Some phrases are hyphenated when used as adjectives, but not when used as adverbs:

> Horn players adjusted out-of-tune notes by hand stopping.
>
> **but**
>
> He sang loudly and out of tune.

Hyphenated names are represented with hyphenated initials:

> J.-J. Rousseau

Prefer en dashes to hyphens in numeric ranges and pitch series (see *2.7: The en dash*).

See also *2.1.1: Compound words and words with prefixes and suffixes*.

2.7 The en dash

The en dash is longer than a hyphen, but shorter than an em dash; its name derives from case-drawer typesetting, when it was the dash the width of an N. It is used rather than a hyphen for date or page ranges:

> 1786–99
>
> 1854–1953
>
> pp. 63–72

It is also used for joining names:

> Strauss–Hofmannsthal correspondence

Use en dashes to join a series of pitches:

> the B♭–A–C–B motive

En dashes are particularly useful as substitutes for hyphens when multi-word compound nouns are modified:

post–World War II culture

In this case, a hyphen would have limited the adjective *post* to *World*; only with the en dash does *post* apply to the whole phrase *World War II*:

Franco-Prussian War–era compositions

non–interest-bearing accounts

When qualifying a century that is used adjectivally, use an en dash to separate the qualifier from the century, and a hyphen to separate the number from the century:

late–19th-century music

pre–18th-century continuo practice

2.8 The em dash

The em dash is the longest commonly used dash, named for being the width of an M. A pair of em dashes is more powerful than commas and more forceful than parentheses for setting off a phrase:

He was—though it bothered him little—universally hated.

When an em dash appears in a title, always capitalize the following word:

Burl Ives: The unauthorized biography—An introduction

In the above example the em dash is used to avoid multiple colons. It can also function as a colon or comma for dramatic emphasis:

He had a plan—a plan that required immediate action.

They were archetypal enemies of the arts—arrogant ignoramuses.

Em dashes are also used to separate one or more subjects from a pronoun that starts a sentence's main clause:

Debussy, Ravel, and Satie—these were the composers she loved.

2.9 The slash

The slash (shill, solidus, virgule) is used for bilingual journal or book titles.

Jazzforschung/Jazz research

It may also be used in certain technical contexts to replace *and*:

tonic/nontonic polarity

Avoid using it to replace *or* (e.g., *he/she, and/or, parent/guardian*).

Do not put spaces around a slash.

Do not use slashes for date or page ranges, or in opus-plus-number designations. Exceptionally, academic years may be designated with a slash (e.g., 2005/06).

2.10 The apostrophe

Singular possessives are always made by tacking *'s* onto the end of the name or word, regardless of its final letter:

Brahms's   Delius's   Boulez's

wrong: Brahms'   Delius'   Boulez'

terribly wrong: Brahm's   Ive's   Boule'z (yes, we have seen these)

Possessives of plurals ending with *s* are made using just an apostrophe:

the Habsburgs' patronage

Rules for apostrophes are different in some languages; English rules should not be forced on them when quoting non-English titles or passages. Also, the British often drop the apostrophe in firm names (Bushmills Distillery, Lloyds of London) and in churches (Saint Andrews).

2.11 Quotation marks

For titles, see *10.1.1: Italics vs. quotation marks*.

2.11.1 Terms

Terms as terms are generally italicized in prose:

the term *sonata form* denotes

in this sense *ballad* implies

Use quotation marks after verbs such as *called* or *labeled* for terms for which the author or speaker does not take responsibility:

called the music "primitive"

labeled him a "barbarian"

2.11.2 Scare quotes

Avoid scare quotes (quotes used for emphasis); they are obtuse.

She argues that a "definitive" method of singing does not exist.

should be

She argues that a definitive method of singing does not exist.

2.11.3 End punctuation with quotation marks

Contrary to common practice, RILM favors precision: Punctuation is only treated as part of a quotation if it actually is. Quotes are closed before end punctuation unless an entire sentence is being quoted:

She was called "the wisest woman in the realm".

He wrote: "This is enough. I'm finished."

2.12 Parentheses and brackets

Parentheses are used for material that is less essential to the sentence than that set off by em dashes or commas:

Most Irish dance tunes (jigs, reels, and hornpipes) have regular, predictable structures.

Some of Goethe's poems (e.g., *Der Schatzgräber*) have been set by several composers.

Brackets are rare. Technically, they should be used within parentheses, but try not to get into a situation that requires this.

> (Labaree's dissertation [1989] provides further examples.)
>> **becomes**
> (Labaree's 1989 dissertation provides further examples.)

The main use of brackets is to indicate editorial interpolations in quotations (see *13.3: Introducing changes*).

See also *3.6: Slang abbreviations*; *5.2.1: Numbering series in sentences*; *10.1.2: Translations*; *16.5: In-text citations and bibliographic formats*.

2.12.1 Parenthetical sentences

Rarely, one or more full sentences may be parenthesized, especially if they present illustrative material. (Parenthetical sentences should never occur within sentences. They should be set off separately, like these.) In general, discursive digressions work better in numbered notes (see *1.4.1: Substantive notes and hyperlinks*).

3. ABBREVIATIONS

3.1 Names of organizations

These should be unabbreviated and in their original languages (see *9.2: Names of organizations*). The second and subsequent times an organization is mentioned its name may be abbreviated if a familiar, commonly used abbreviation exists. If you will be using an abbreviated form, include it in parentheses after the initial use of the full name.

> The American Musicological Society (AMS) meets annually. Past locations of AMS meetings include . . .

Some organizations, such as UNESCO, are primarily known by their acronyms; it is rarely necessary to spell out their full names.

Names of organizations that do not have commonly used abbreviations may be referred to generically the second and subsequent times they appear:

> The Institut za Etnologiju i Folkloristiku in Zagreb has been carrying out large-scale systematic fieldwork on Istrian traditional music since its founding in 1947. The institute's archives comprise . . .

3.2 St. and SS.

St. and *SS.* are the abbreviations for Saint and Saints in all cases when referring to the human beings, since these references are in English. Place names, surnames, and institutions vary in usage; do not force standardized forms on them.

Antoine de Saint-Exupéry	Sankt Augustin
Jill St. John	Santa Maria del Fiore
Pascale Saint-André	SS. Giovanni e Paolo
Saint-Amand	St. Catherine
Saint-Cyr-l'École	St. Louis, Missouri
San Francisco	Yves Saint Laurent

3.3 Punctuating abbreviations

In British English, periods are not used after abbreviations comprising the first and last letters of words:

Dr Williams   Mr Pierson   St Bartholomews Church

In U.S. English, periods are used after most abbreviations of single words:

ca. 1300   op. 111   Dr. Salk

Exceptions include units of measurement and scientific and technical terms:

60 dB   440 Hz   78 rpm

Periods (no space) are used for most two-letter acronyms:

E.U.   G.E.   U.S.

Again, the exceptions tend to be technical and technological terms:

CD (for *compact disc*)

AM (for *amplitude modulation*)

AP (for *absolute pitch*)

Do not use periods or spaces in acronyms of three or more letters:

BWV   IAML   UNESCO

   but

B.C.E., to match C.E. (see *5.3: Dates*)

No space is needed between personal initials or between two-letter acronyms. Use one space after the initials:

C.P.E. Bach   U.N. mandate

Do not put a space between a one-letter abbreviation and a number:

The G-minor symphony, K.440, may be Mozart's best-known work.

No space is used after *b.* or *d.*, unless a place comes before the date.

Copland (d. New York 1990) spoke for all America.

Other abbreviations are followed by one space:

> string quartet, op. 131 Johannes Kloster (fl. 1560–85)
>
> *Tractatus de musica* (ca. 1320)

Exceptionally, by analogy with Mozart's *K.* numbers and Schubert's *D.* numbers, Haydn's *Hob.* is closed up:

> Hob.XII:4

See also *10.3: Opus and catalogue numbers.*

3.4 Et al. and etc.

Et al. is short for *et alii* (and others); etc. is short for *et cetera* (and other things). The former is used only for people; the latter is used for things, places, ideas, and so on. They are always preceded by a comma and a space. They are never italicized.

Avoid using them in formal prose: Use their prose equivalents instead. They may be used in parenthetical situations.

3.5 I.e. and e.g.

I.e. is short for *id est* (that is); *e.g.* is short for *exempli gratia* (for example). Use *i.e.* when what follows is a clarification, and use *e.g.* when what follows is one or more possible illustrations:

> The accompanying instruments (i.e., the tablā and tambūrā) . . .
>
> Ravel's excursions into exoticism (e.g., *Shéhérazade*) . . .

I.e. and *e.g.* are always followed by a comma and are never italicized.

As with *et al.* and *etc.*, reserve these for parenthetical situations: Do not use them in formal prose.

3.6 Slang abbreviations

Some slang abbreviations, such as *a.k.a.* (for *also known as*) are common in journalistic writing; they are avoided in scholarly writing. *A.k.a.* may be replaced by parentheses.

> They met McKinley Morganfield (Muddy Waters) in 1941.

4. PLURALS

Standard plural abbreviations may be used:

mm.   nos.   opp.   pp.

Plurals of assimilated words are in English style:

concertos, **not** concerti

librettos

virtuosos

opuses (Try to get around this one, though; it is unappealing.)

However, where a foreign plural is as common as the familiar singular form, or is listed first in a standard English dictionary, it may be retained:

alumni	lieder
concerti grossi	media
curricula	opere serie
Festschriften	opere buffe
hazanim	syllabi
klezmorim	topoi

Criteria is the plural of *criterion*.

Data is the plural of *datum*.

Commata is the plural of *comma* (the interval, not the punctuation).

4.1 Non-Western plurals

Where it is not easy to deduce the singular from the plural, the singular may be given thus:

professional epic singers, known as *shuʿarā* (singular, *shāʿir*)

Non-Western terms that appear in standard English dictionaries may be considered assimilated:

gamelans   kotos   ragas

If you add an *s* to a nonassimilated non-Western term that has no plural form, do not distinguish it typographically from the term:

> Lou Harrison composed several gendings. (**not** gending-s, *gending*s)

If you are confident that your readers know the language in question, there is no need to add the *s*.

See also *7.1: Terms*.

5. NUMBERS

5.1 Figures vs. words

Cardinal and ordinal numbers up to and including ten are spelled out; 11 and above are figures (except as discussed below and in *5.5: Times of day* and *10.2: Generic titles*):

> fourth movement
>
> ten maids a-milking
>
> Schoenberg's 12-tone compositions
>
> nearly 300 years later

Ordinal numbers greater than *tenth*, when they do not begin a sentence, consist of a figure and a two-letter suffix:

> It was the 158th piece Telemann wrote that month.

For multiples of 1,000,000, spell out the appropriate unit and follow the first rule above for the multiple:

> two million   48 billion   306 trillion

Act, scene, chapter, page, opus, and catalogue numbers are always arabic figures:

> act 2, scene 3
>
> chapter 1, page 2
>
> Haydn's string quartet op. 76, no. 3
>
> *Gretchen am Spinnrade*, D.118

Numbered movements are identified with ordinal numbers, spelled out:

> in the third movement of his string quartet no. 5
>
> **not**
>
> in movement no. 3 of his string quartet no. 5
>
> **or**
>
> in movement 3

Measurements, statistics, and model numbers should always be figures:

> washed with a .2% solution of sulfuric acid
>
> using a 50 mm bore

Centuries are usually rendered as figures:

> 2nd century B.C.E.
>
> 8th century
>
> 21st century

A cardinal or ordinal number at the beginning of a sentence must be written out, so try to avoid this where it would be awkward:

> Five students . . .
>
> Twenty-third on the list . . .
>
> Eighteenth-century dances . . .
>
> In all, 2346 songs . . . (to avoid spelling out the number)

When citing titles, leave numbers and dates however they are printed.

When translating titles, conform the translation to English style.

> title: *Franz Födermayr zum 60. Geburtstag*
>
> translation: Franz Födermayr on his 60th birthday
>
> title: *Eberhard Würzl zum achtzigsten Geburtstag*
>
> translation: Eberhard Würzl on his 80th birthday

5.2 Punctuation

5.2.1 Numbering series in sentences

When using numbers to organize major points (do not use letters or roman numerals), enclose them in parentheses and separate the points with semicolons:

> Four trends emerged in the traditional music of Yugoslavia between 1960 and 1965: (1) retention of existing forms, with minor changes in melodies; (2) structural changes in the music system; (3) acceptance of essentially new phenomena and their adaptation; and (4) newly composed songs (lyrical poems with melodies that contain traditional elements, new long narrative poems, chronicles, and instrumental and vocal compositions).

Caution: This technique is overused. Always think about whether the passage would read more smoothly without the numbers:

> Stravinsky manipulates motivic material through variation (*Le sacre du printemps*), repetition (*L'oiseau de feu*), and inversion (*In memoriam Dylan Thomas*).
>
> **not**
>
> Stravinsky manipulates motivic material in three different ways: (1) variation in *Le sacre du printemps*; (2) repetition in *L'oiseau de feu*; and (3) inversion in *In memoriam Dylan Thomas*.

5.2.2 Large numbers

Do not use commas in figures of four digits or fewer; use them otherwise:

> 10,000 Maniacs   5000 listeners

5.3 Dates

Write dates thus (day, if any, before month, month before year, and no commas at all):

> *Concierto de Aranjuez* premiered on 9 November 1940.
>
> Copland completed *Piano variations* in August 1930.

Do not repeat the first two digits in date ranges within a century:

> 1823–87

Retain zeros for early years of centuries:

> 1801–09

A question mark goes after the questionable date:

> Umm Kulthūm (1904?–75)

If words introduce a date range, words (rather than an en dash) must be used in the middle as well (see *2.7: The en dash*):

> a survey of concerts from 1956 through 1959
>
> **not**
>
> a survey of concerts from 1956–59

22

When describing a decade, do not use apostrophes:

San Francisco in the 1960s
not
San Francisco in the 1960's

A recent trend in scholarship supports replacing *A.D.* (*Anno Domini*, Year of Our Lord) and *B.C.* (Before Christ) with *C.E.* (Common Era) and *B.C.E.* (Before the Common Era), respectively. This practice eliminates the problem of applying Christian-centered terminology where it would be inappropriate.

Unlike *A.D.*, which precedes the year, *C.E.* and *B.C.E.* follow it:

66 C.E.   492 B.C.E.

Use *C.E.* sparingly, usually only when it closes a range that began before the year 1 C.E. or in a very early century. If the topic is musical practices in a 9th-century Saxon abbey, *C.E.* is not needed.

To avoid ambiguity, century redundancy is required in B.C.E. dates—for example, 327–325 B.C.E. (Abridging the second date would confound 325 B.C.E. with 25 B.C.E.)

When referring to Asian dynasties, include date ranges:

The earliest information on music in Korea dates from the Gogu'ryeo dynasty (37 B.C.E.–668 C.E.).

When source documents give dates according to the Julian calendar, convert the dates to the Gregorian (C.E.) calendar, but give the Julian ones in parentheses:

Stevan Mokranjac was born on 9 January 1856 (Julian: 28 December 1855).

Otherwise, when a date is given in an alternative system it is followed by the Gregorian version in parentheses:

Abū Ma'šar began his scholarly career at the caliphate court at al-Ma'mūn between 199 and 219 A.H. (813–833 C.E.).

5.4 Page ranges

Use a comma to separate page ranges from individual page numbers or other ranges in bibliographic data:

> 67–71, 75
>
> 459–463, 495–501

When citing an article published in two or more languages in the same publication, use a semicolon between page ranges.

If several nearly adjacent page ranges are indicated (e.g., for an article in a magazine with full-page advertisements), simplify and cite one inclusive range only.

5.5 Times of day

Times of day in full, half, and quarter hours are spelled out:

> They expected the meeting to continue until half past three.
>
> The family always ate lunch at twelve o'clock.
>
> The performance ended around nine-thirty.

But numerals are used (with zeros for full hours) when the exact moment of time is emphasized:

> The program is televised at 2:30 in the afternoon.
>
> Liftoff occurred at 11:05 a.m.

In Britain a period is used between the hour and minutes rather than a colon.

Abbreviations for time of day (a.m., p.m.) are lowercase. Do not use these abbreviations with *morning, afternoon, evening, night*, or *o'clock*.

> 10:45 a.m.
>
> 10:45 in the morning
>
> ten o'clock in the evening

Do not include *12:00* with the words *noon* or *midnight*.

5.6 Roman vs. arabic

When citing books that have more than one level of volume or series numbers, differentiate them by using roman numerals for the larger grouping:

> Händel, Georg Friedrich. *Israel in Egypt, HWV 54.* Hallische Händel-Ausgabe: Kritische Gesamtausgabe. I: Oratorien und große Kantaten, 14. Kassel: Bärenreiter, 1999.

Otherwise, prefer arabic in prose. For example, use arabic for act and scene numbers of stage works:

> act 2, scene 1

6. SPELLING

6.1 U.S. conventions

If you are using U.S. spelling conventions, stick to them:

theater, **not** theatre

center, **not** centre

color, **not** colour

practice, **not** practise

behavior, **not** behaviour

analyze, **not** analyse

traveled, **not** travelled

memoir, **not** memoire

premiere, **not** première

The most notable exception is *repertoire*, which need not be translated to *repertory* for Western classical topics. *Repertory* is preferred for ethno-musicological topics.

Do not change the spelling of an organization:

American Ballet Theatre, New York

Royal Centre, Nottingham

Opinions differ regarding *catalog* vs. *catalogue, dialog* vs. *dialogue*, and so on. While the shorter forms may be considered U.S. usage, many U.S. writers and publishers (including RILM) favor the longer forms. In general, *dialog* is preferred in computer-related words (e.g., *dialog box*).

6.2 Common problems

a cappella, **not** a capella

defense, **not** defence

improvise, **not** improvize

judgment, **not** judgement

supersede, **not** supercede

supplement, **not** suppliment

Discrete means noncontinuous; *discreet* means prudent.

To *affect* something is to have an effect on it; to *effect* something is to bring it about.

A *complement* completes; a *compliment* honors.

6.3 Transcribing dialect and pronunciation

The benefits and disadvantages of transcribing a person's singing or speech with variant spellings to indicate particularities of dialect or pronunciation have been discussed at length by scholars working with a variety of topics, from ballads to blues. The main drawback in transcribing pronunciation is that it can make the singer or speaker appear unsophisticated or foolish, particularly when it is framed by scholarly prose. In most cases, nonstandard pronunciation may be disregarded without misrepresenting intent or spirit. As noted in *13.3: Introducing changes*, the wording of quotations—including the use of contractions—must not be altered; details of pronunciation, however, should only be indicated if they are themselves an object of study.

7. ITALIC VS. ROMAN TYPE

See also *2.11.1: Terms*; *10: Titles*.

7.1 Terms

Names of peoples, places, instruments, genres (music or dance), organizations, and political or aesthetic trends are not italicized. No clear rules can be formulated for determining which terms for instruments and genres may be considered assimilated among scholars who write about music, so it is best to treat them all the same way.

> Debussy brought impressionism into the realm of music.
>
> He plays the jembe to accompany manjani dancing.
>
> The Théâtre National de l'Opéra-Comique was founded in 1714.

A number of non-Western terms now appear in standard English dictionaries; these are generally treated as assimilated words.

gamelan	raga
koto	sitar
mbira	tabla
mridangam	tala

However, in ethnomusicological writings terms are given standardized transliterations (see *12.3: Transliteration*):

mṛdaṅgam	sitār
rāga	tāla

Other unassimilated words are italicized. Any word found in a standard English dictionary is considered assimilated. If the word is used repeatedly, only italicize its first appearance.

> *Jouissance* is a driving force in film music. Elements associated with jouissance include . . .

Occasionally it will make sense to italicize a foreign generic term to differentiate it from an English word with the same spelling:

> His son became a famous *son* singer.

A few phrases of foreign origin that do appear in English dictionaries (e.g., *a cappella*, *a priori*) are italicized solely to make them easier to read in prose.

Occasionally a term may be italicized the first time it appears to signal that it is being used in a specialized way. It does not have to be a foreign word. This is an extension of the rule given in *2.11.1: Terms*.

> The three main types of development are *motivic*, *harmonic*, and *contrapuntal*.

See also *4.1: Non-Western plurals*.

7.2 Legal cases

Names of legal cases are italicized and, contrary to usage elsewhere, *v.* is used rather than *vs.*

> *Roe v. Wade*

7.3 Ships and trains

The name of a ship is italicized, but not the article or title (USS, HMS, etc.) preceding it. Names of trains or train routes are in roman type.

> Longfellow's poem begins with a scene onboard the *Hesprus*.
>
> Many Pitcairn residents descended from the HMS *Bounty* mutineers.
>
> Blind Willie McTell also celebrated the B. & O. line in song.

8. CAPITALIZATION

Two styles are used for capitalization when dealing with more than one word: headline style and sentence style.

In headline style, articles (a, an, the), conjunctions (and, or), and prepositions (to, from, through, unless they are emphasized or used as modifiers or conjunctions) are lowercase; other major words (nouns, pronouns, verbs, modifiers) are capitalized; and the first and last words are invariably capitalized.

> Ford to New York: Drop Dead

In sentence style, only those words that would be capitalized in normal prose are uppercase. Work titles are always in sentence style.

> *How Tom beat Captain Najork and his hired sportsmen*

8.1 When to capitalize

Genre and cultural movement names where there is no ambiguity are lowercase (sonata, futurism), but capitalized where confusion could result (Mass, Renaissance).

Generic designations of pieces and scenes are lowercase (the mad scenes in bel canto opera, Beethoven's fifth symphony).

Fixed-though-informal English names of particular things, such as scenes and manuscripts, are capitalized in headline style: Articles (*a, an, the*), conjunctions (*an, or*), and prepositions (*to, from, through,* unless they are emphasized or used as modifiers or conjunctions) are lowercase; other major words (nouns, pronouns, verbs, modifiers) are capitalized; and the first and last words are invariably capitalized (the Mad Scene in *Lucia di Lammermoor*, the Dance of the Seven Veils; the Siena Lute Book).

Act and scene designations are lowercase, with arabic numerals.

Names of software (Microsoft Word), copyrighted tests (Adolescent Perception Test), and methods and techniques whose names are copyrighted or otherwise legally owned (Feldenkreis Method, Alexander Technique) are capitalized in headline style.

Names of organizations or institutions (Library of Congress, International Musicological Society) are capitalized in headline style.

Genericized English names (The Rock of Gibraltar, St. Peter's Basilica) are capitalized in headline style.

Ongoing broadcast programs or series (All Things Considered) are capitalized in headline style, because they are considered to be institutions. A single episode of a broadcast series, or a one-time program, is italicized and treated as a work (see *10.1: True titles*).

The titles of academic courses (Introduction to Music) are capitalized in headline style.

Capitalize a performing group's institutional name in headline style (Carter Family, Currence Brothers). Do not capitalize if the family is not a formal group (Seeger family, Bach family).

Brand names that are registered trademarks are capitalized in headline style if the reference is specific. For a generic reference, substitute a generic term.

> Kleenex, **prefer** tissue
>
> Xerox, **prefer** photocopy

Occasionally brand names have eccentric capitalization (e.g., iPod); these are retained.

Acronyms are capitalized (BBC, IAML); in rare cases, lowercase initials are included (RIdIM for Répertoire International d'Iconographie Musicale).

See also *10: Titles*; for foreign languages, see *12.2: Capitalization*.

8.2 Examples

act 1, scene 2	Classic (historical)
ars nova	expressionism
baroque (general)	Gothic cathedral
Baroque (historical)	gothic novel
Bible	Gradual (as liturgy)
biblical	gradual (as book)
Bowen Technique	Harlem Renaissance
classic (general)	impressionism

Internet	Suzuki Method
Laban Movement Analysis	trecento (general)
Muzička Akademija	Trecento (style period)
new age music	verbunkos
New German School	waltz
renaissance (general)	World Wide Web (or Web)
Renaissance (historical)	website
Second Viennese School	western (general)
Stomp Dance	Western (cultural)

8.3 Assimilated German nouns

Assimilated German nouns are not capitalized:

baryton	lieder
frankfurter	singspiel
gestalt (but Gestalt therapy)	urtext
glockenspiel	weltanschauung
hamburger	weltschmerz
leitmotiv	zeitgeist

8.4 Slang names and racial epithets

Derogatory or slang names for peoples are never capitalized. Such terms should only be used when absolutely necessary—for example, in discussions of racial or cultural prejudices.

honkies	krauts

9. NAMES

9.1 Names of people

9.1.1 Spelling

Personal names are given with their original spelling and diacritics. Transliteration should follow ISO standards (see *12.3: Transliteration*).

Seosamh Ó hÉanaí

Sergej Sergeevič Prokof'ev

Trần Văn Khê

Persons who lived long as expatriates may have their names spelled otherwise:

Diaghilev	Nijinsky
Liszt	Schoenberg
Lully	Stravinsky

but: Händel, not Handel nor Haendel

Medieval or other persons known only by first name and father's name, region, or an adjective should be given in full form (first name followed by region) the first time they are mentioned:

Abu Naṣr al-Fārābī	Guillaume de Machaut
Guido of Arezzo	Mikołaj z Radomia

Common shorter forms may be used thereafter:

al-Fārābī	Machaut
Guido	Mikołaj

9.1.2 Alphabetization

9.1.2.1 Married names

For women with a married name preceded by an unmarried name (unhyphenated), use the married name, unless she publishes under the compound surname. Always use the compound surname if it is hyphenated.

Callegari Hill, Laura	Seeger, Ruth Crawford

9.1.2.2 *Jr., III*, etc.

When these are part of personal names (as opposed to titles), alphabetize thus:

Gordy, Berry, Jr.   Hammerstein, Oscar, II

For titles with roman numerals, see *9.1.4: Epithets and honorifics*.

9.1.2.3 Compound names

Hyphenated names always appear under the first surname:

Mendelssohn-Bartholdy, Felix

Alphabetization of non-hyphenated surnames varies. Consult the International Federation of Library Associations and Institutions (IFLA) *Names of persons: National uses for entry in catalogues* (München: Saur, 1996) for any question not answered here.

Dutch compound surnames, including those with prefixes, are alphabetized by the first part of the compound:

Slicher van Bath, Bernard   Goes van Naters, M. van der

Italian compound surnames, including those with prefixes, are also alphabetized by the first part of the surname:

Rosmini Serbati, Antonio   Sala di Felice, Elena

Portuguese compound surnames are alphabetized under the last part:

Baptista Filho, Zito   Lima, João de Souza

Filho (Brazilian) means Junior; it is not a true surname. *Júnior* (always spelled out) should be treated like Filho as shown above.

Russian, Ukrainian, and Belorussian names consist of a forename, patronymic, and surname. They are alphabetized by surname:

Čajkovskij, Pëtr Il'ič

Čajkovskaja, Antonina Miljukova

34

Spanish compound surnames, including those with prefixes, are alphabetized under the first part of the surname:

García Lorca, Federico   Calderón de la Barca, Pedro

9.1.2.4 Prefixes

U.S. and British names are alphabetized under the prefix, even if the country of origin of the name does otherwise:

De Zeeuw, Anne Marie

Although this name is of Dutch origin, and would be alphabetized under the surname if she were Dutch, since she is from the U.S. her name is alphabetized the U.S. way.

Belgian surnames with prefixes follow French rules for French names, but U.S. or British rules for Dutch names:

Van Maldere, Pierre   Vos, Luc de

Canadian surnames with prefixes follow French rules for French names and U.S. or British rules for English names.

Dutch surnames with prefixes are alphabetized by the part following the prefix.

Borren, Charles van den   Kinderen, Anton der

French surnames with prefixes are alphabetized under the article if the prefix is an article, an article plus a preposition, or a contraction of an article and a preposition; alphabetize under the surname if the prefix is just a preposition:

Alembert, Henri d'   Le Cordier, Roland

Des Forêts, Louis-René   La Grange, Henry-Louis de

Du Barry, Marie   Nerval, Gérard de

Irish surnames with prefixes are alphabetized under the prefix. Irish prefixes include the masculine *Ó* and *Mac* and the feminine *Ní* and *Uí* (the Anglicized prefixes *Mc* and *O'* are ungendered):

MacMathúna, Ciarán   O'Connor, Sinéad

McCormack, John   Ó Riada, Seán

Ní Mhaonaigh, Mairéad   Uí Chróinín, Éilís

German surnames with prefixes are alphabetized under the part following the prefix:

Beethoven, Ludwig van   Schiller, Friedrich von

Hagen, Friedrich von der

Italian surnames are alphabetized by prefix, except for pre–19th-century names with prefixes indicating noble descent (*de, de', degli, dei,* and *de li*) and surnames including a place name by which a person is usually identified:

Dall' Ongaro, Francesca   Medici, Francesco de'

Di Benedetto, Vincenzo   Palestrina, Giovanni Pierluigi da

South African surnames with prefixes, even those of Dutch or French origin, are alphabetized by the prefix.

Van Biljon, Ernest Hendrik   De Villiers, Dirkie

Spanish surnames with prefixes comprising only an article are alphabetized by the prefix:

Las Heras, Manuel Antonio

When the prefix consists of a preposition only, or a preposition and an article, alphabetize by the part following the prefix:

Adelid y Gurréa, Marcial de   Vega, Francisco de la

Santos, Rafael de los

Summary

Da [Italian surname], see Da; see also exceptions above

De [Belgian/South African surname], see De

De [Dutch surname], see surname

De [French surname], see surname

De' [Italian surname], see De'; see also exceptions above

De [Spanish surname], see surname

De La [French /Spanish surname], see La

De La [Spanish surname], see surname

Del [Spanish surname], see surname

Di [Italian surname], see Di

Du [French surname], see Du

Van [Belgian surname], see Van

Van [Dutch/German surname], see surname

Van [South African surname], see Van

Van Der [Belgian surname], see Van Der

Van Der [Dutch surname], see surname

Van Der [South African surname], see Van Der

Von [German surname], see surname

9.1.2.5 Other considerations for particular languages

Arabic names before the 19th century are varied; when in doubt, render them without commas or inversions:

'Abd al-Qāder al-Marāghī

Modern names may be inverted:

al-Farrān, Ibrāhīm

Such names are alphabetized under the element following the particle. Therefore, some authorities prefer to invert the name thus:

Farrān, Ibrāhīm al-

East and Southeast Asian names are normally not inverted. The main exceptions involve Western given names; these appear before the surname in prose, and they are inverted for alphabetization. For example, Margaret Leng Tan is alphabetized as Tan, Margaret Leng.

- **Chinese, Korean, and Vietnamese names** comprise a surname (usually one syllable) followed by a given name (usually two syllables). In China, names are never hyphenated; they are usually hyphenated in Taiwan and Hong Kong (and, occasionally, in Malaysia and Singapore), with the second syllable uppercase for surnames (e.g., Ssu-Ma, Au-Yeong) and lowercase for given names (e.g., T'ien-hua, You-ch'ien). Korean given names are usually two hyphenated syllables, with the second syllable lowercase. Vietnamese given names are written as separate names, both capitalized.

Ouyang Jinxing (following mainland Chinese standard)

Au-Yeong Kam-sing (Chinese not from mainland)

Kim Hae-suk (Korean)

Trần Văn Khê (Vietnamese)

- **Japanese names** are not hyphenated. The honorific suffixes *-san*, *-sama*, and *-sensei* should not be treated as part of a name.

- **Malay names** (found in several parts of Southeast Asia) comprise one or two given names followed by the father's name, which may also consist of two names. Malays do not use surnames unless the name is of some other origin (such as Western or Chinese; follow the rules for the original language). There is sometimes a particle such as *bin* between the given names and the father's name. Malay names are not inverted.

Siti Zainon Ismail

Hassan bin Abdul Majid

Inon Shaharuddin Abdul Rahman

- **South Asian names** are difficult to standardize. India alone has some 325 recognized languages; add the other countries of the Indian subcontinent and the challenge of consistency becomes quite daunting. For authors who write in English, use the form they use, even if it differs from other renditions of the same name (Krishnamoorthy, Krishnamurthi, Krishnamurthy, Krishnamurti, etc.); for others, prefer the applicable transliteration (Kiruṣṇamūrtti, Kiruṭṭiṇamūrtti, Kṛṣṇamūrti, etc.).

Hungarian names may be found with the surname as the first element: for example, Bodnár István. Since Bodnár is the surname, the name appears as István Bodnár in prose, and it is alphabetized as Bodnár, István.

Icelandic names comprise of a given name followed by a patronymic. They are alphabetized by given name.

Aðalgeir Kristjánsson   Helga Guðmundsdóttir

9.1.3 Name changes, pseudonyms, and sobriquets

For people who permanently changed their names when moving to a new country or for religious or other reasons, use the new name instead of the old. However, if a person is known by a pseudonym or sobriquet, use their birth name with the pseudonym or sobriquet in parentheses in bibliographic listings.

> Marx, Arthur (Harpo), **not** Adolph; he changed his given name.
>
> Owens, Dana (Queen Latifah)
>
> Pujol, Joseph (Le Pétomane)

9.1.4 Epithets and honorifics

Epithets are preceded by *the*:

> the publisher Ottaviano Petrucci
>
> the entertainer Lady Bunny
>
> the novelist Bulwer-Lytton

Names of popes, early saints, and emperors are given in the familiar English or Latin form (John, Pius), or a national form if it is the familiar one (Franz Josef).

Pope, *King*, and *Saint* may be dropped (e.g., Clement XIII, Augustine); this practice is not required, but it is more sophisticated. See also *3.2: St. and SS.*

A Pope's secular name may be included the first time he is mentioned:

> Innocent XI Odeschalchi
>
> Benedict XVI Ratzinger

In general, refer to titled people using the highest title they received. Of course, if you are discussing their life before they were so titled, it will make sense to use whatever their name or title was at the time.

> Augustine
>
> Charles II, Holy Roman Emperor
>
> Charles II, King of England
>
> John XXIII

Titles and honorifics such as *Doctor*, *Sir*, and *Dame* may be omitted in most kinds of writing (exceptions may include tributes, obituaries, etc.).

Sir and *Dame* are only followed by a given name, even in abbreviated references:

Joan Sutherland	Sutherland
Dame Joan Sutherland	Dame Joan

9.1.4.1 Non-Western honorifics

Many cultures bestow terms of respect on accomplished musicians, teachers, and other worthy persons. Although these terms may be capitalized, they are not a formal part of the person's name, and they should be omitted in scholarly writing. Examples include *Pandit* and *Ustad* in India, *Bapak*, *Ibu*, and *Ki* in Indonesia, and the suffixes *-san* and *-sensei* in Japan.

9.1.5 Incomplete and descriptive names

When only one name element is known for a historical person who undoubtedly had others, use that name, with an honorific or title if one is commonly associated with that person. For example, the 18th-century English choreographer is known in sources only as "Mr. Isaac". Do not add titles or honorifics without precedents in sources. Names with only one element are common in several non-Western cultures; do not add anything to them.

Kālidāsa	Sumarsam

Historical visual artists who are known only through their works may be known by temporary names such as Master, followed by a place name, initials, or a description of a work. Use the English form *Master* regardless of the artist's nationality.

> Master of Flémalles
>
> Master of the Embroidered Foliage

Rare exceptions are names of artists known by certain stylistic features:

> Painter of the Long Overfalls

Temporary names of painters of Attic ceramics should be capitalized and in the following form:

> Andokides Painter, **not** the painter of Andokides
>
> Pig Painter, **not** the painter of Schweinerei

9.1.6 First names and initials

The first names of famous persons may be omitted unless there is a good chance of confusion. If confusion is likely, give the first name. For famous families, give the initial(s):

Bach (J.S. is assumed)	D. Scarlatti
C.P.E. Bach	G. Gabrieli

It is a sign of respect to drop first names. Some very famous persons seem to always be stuck with their first names (or initials) for no good reason; it is better to drop them:

Eliot's *Four quartets*	Strauss's *Elektra*

Famous women and nonclassical musicians should also go without their first names:

Fitzgerald's scat singing

settings of Dickinson's poems

9.1.7 Middle names and patronymics

Patronymics for Slavic names should always be included in bibliographic listings. Other types of middle names are also often included in bibliographies, but middle names of either variety are seldom needed in prose passages.

9.1.8 Dates

In scholarly writing, a person's birth and death dates may be included in parentheses the first time the name appears; do not do this for famous names. Dates may also be used to distinguish persons with the same name.

9.1.9 Scriptural, early, legendary, and mythological names

In prose, these are given in the forms most commonly found in English writings:

Apollo	Mohammed
Don Juan	Moses
Krishna	Plato

9.2 Names of organizations

Organization or institution names are given in the original language, in roman type, and capitalized in headline style (see *8.1: When to capitalize*):

> Accademia Filarmonica
>
> American Federation of Labor
>
> Bibliothèque Nationale de France
>
> Hrvatska Akademija Znanosti i Umjetnosti
>
> Teatral'noe Učilišče
>
> Ediciones Mexicanas de Música
>
> Libreria Musicale Italiana

For non-European languages, an English translation may be given in parentheses, especially if the organization is known internationally by the English name:

> Sainō Kyōiku Ongaku Gakkō (Talent Education Music School)

Treat ongoing broadcast programs and series as institutions:

> Absolutely Fabulous   The Ed Sullivan Show

A single program is treated as a work (see *10.1: True titles*):

> *Live aid*
>
> *The art of the violin*, from the Great Performances series

Exhibitions and conferences are considered temporary organizations.

> Degas and the Dance (Philadelphia, 2003)

Organizations whose names have changed should be referred to with the appropriate name for the time period under discussion; the current name may follow in parentheses.

Religious, royal, and international institutions may be in a source language, in English, or in an otherwise familiar form. If given as one of a genre (i.e., a name plus an English word or words), they should be capitalized nevertheless (e.g., Fürstenfeld Abbey). Never add *Church* to Germanic forms containing that word (e.g., Frauenkirche, Vrouwkerk); do not add *St.* to Germanic churches (e.g., Thomaskirche, Nikolaikirche).

If a name is given, even if not in the original language, put *Church* or *Temple*, capitalized. If no name is given, however, use lowercase:

The Church of Jesus Christ of Latter-Day Saints

The church on Broadway and 10th Street

Shri Akshar Purushottam Swaminarayan Temple

The Hindu temples in Tamil Nadu

For abbreviations, see *3.1: Names of organizations.*

9.3 Names of places

For punctuation with place names, see *2.2.2: Place names.*

9.3.1 Country and region names

Names of countries and regions are given in English:

Central African Republic	Pacific Rim
Ivory Coast	Silesia

9.3.2 Directional adjectives

The terms *North, South, West*, etc., are always uppercase in place names. *Central* is uppercase for a continent and lowercase when applied to a country. *Eastern, western*, etc., are uppercase if they are part of a region's proper name or a recognized subsection of a supranational region or continent. Otherwise, they are lowercase.

Central Asia	southern France
Eastern Europe	West Africa

9.3.3 States and provinces

Write out the names of states and provinces in prose. When abbreviating them, use the standard abbreviations, not the postal abbreviations.

9.3.4 City and town names

If there is a prevailing, familiar English name for a place (e.g., Milan), use it rather than the true place name (e.g., Milano). Otherwise, call it whatever the people who live there call it. Avoid outdated appellations such as Leghorn or Muscovy.

In general, use the current name of a town or city. Where appropriate, put historical names in parentheses:

>She spent her formative years in St. Petersburg (then Petrograd).

Places with two current, legal, familiar names (this is unusual) can have both (e.g., Turku/Åbo).

9.3.5 A partial list of cities with alternate names

Bold forms are preferred. However, for publisher listings in citations, give the city name the way the publisher has printed it.

Current name	English	Older names	Other forms
Antwerpen/ Anvers	**Antwerp**		Anversa, Amberes
Athínai	**Athens**		Athenae
Basel/Bâle		Basle	Basilea
Bolzano/Bozen			
Bratislava		Pressburg	Pozsony, Pressburgo, Požun
Braunschweig	Brunswick (obs.)		
Brno		Brünn	
Brugge	**Bruges**		Brujas
Bruxelles/ Brussel	**Brussels**		Bruselas
Bydgoszcz		Bromberg	
Chennai	Madras		
Dilli	Delhi		
Firenze	**Florence**		Florenz, Florencia
Gdańsk		Danzig	

Current name	English	Older names	Other forms
Genève/Genf	**Geneva**		Ginevra, Ginebra
Genova	**Genoa**		Gênes
Gent	**Ghent**		Gante, Gaunt, Gand
's-Gravenhage	**The Hague**		Den Haag, La Haya, L'Aia
Hannover	**Hanover**		Honovre
Kaliningrad		Königsberg	
Karlovy Vary		Karlsbad	
København	**Copenhagen**		Copenhague, Cupenhagen
Kolkata	Calcutta		
Köln	**Cologne**		Colonia
Konstanz	**Constance**		Constanza
Kraków	**Cracow**	Krakau	Cracovie, Cracovia
Kyjiv	**Kiev**		
Laknau	Lucknow		
Legnica		Liegnitz	
Legnickie Pole		Wahlstatt	
Lisboa	**Lisbon**		Lisbonne, Lisbona, Lissabon
Livorno	Leghorn (obs.)		
Luzern	**Lucerne**		Lucerno, Lucerna
L'viv			Lemberg, Lvów, L'vov
Lyon	Lyons		Luydunum
Mantova	**Mantua**		
Milano	**Milan**		Mailand

Current name	English	Older names	Other forms
Montréal	**Montreal**		
Moskva	**Moscow**		Moskau, Mosca, Moscú
Mumbai	Bombay		
München	**Munich**		Monaco, Mónaco
Nai Dilli	New Delhi		
Nürnberg	**Nuremberg**		
Oostend/Ostend	**Ostende**		Ostenda
Ošwięcim		Auschwitz	
Padova	**Padua**		
Pinang (Malaysia)	**George Town**		
Praha	**Prague**	Prag	Praga
Pune	Poona		
al-Qāhira	**Cairo**		
Québec	**Quebec**		
Roma	**Rome**		
Sankt-Peterburg	**St. Petersburg**		Leningrad, Petrograd
Slavkov			Austerlitz
Strasbourg		Straßburg	Estrasburgo, Strasburgo
Szczecin		Stettin	
Thanjavur	Tanjore		
Thessaloníki	Thessalonika, Salonika	Therma	Thessalonique, Salonika, Selanik
Thiruvanan-thapuram	Trivandrum		
Torino	**Turin**		
Trento	**Trent**		Trente

46

Current name	English	Older names	Other forms
Trier	Treves	Trèves	
Turku/Åbo	Turku/Åbo		Turku (Åbo); Åbo/Turku
Varanasi	Benares		
Venezia	**Venice**		Venedig, Venecija, Venise
Warszawa	**Warsaw**	Warschau	Varsovie, Varsovia, Varsavia
Wien	**Vienna**		Viena, Bécs, Beč, Dunaj, Rakúsko
Wroclaw		Breslau	
Yerẃšalayim/ al-Quds	**Jerusalem**		
Zürich	Zurich		Zurigo
Zweibrücken		Deuxponts	

9.3.7 Geographic adjectives

Catalonian is strictly for geographical use; For culture, language, and persons, use *Catalan*.

Use *Filipino*, not *Philippine*.

When referring to a person or thing from the United States, use *U.S.*, not *American*.

Use *British* only when referring to the whole United Kingdom; otherwise use *English*, *Scottish*, and so on, as appropriate.

Use *Hispanic* only when referring to cultural heritage; for peoples of the Americas, use *Latino*.

47

10. TITLES

In prose references, work titles may be followed by parenthetical dates when they are useful to the reader. Do not add them if they are irrelevant to the discussion.

10.1 True titles

True (nongeneric) titles are given in their original language and, with the exception of German titles, with sentence-style capitalization (see *8.1: When to capitalize*). Only the first word in a title or subtitle and subsequent proper names are capitalized. Original punctuation, abbreviations, etc., are retained:

> *Mr. Gilfil's love story*
>
> *Das Lied von der Erde*
>
> *Le marteau sans maître*
>
> *Psalmes, sonets, & songs*

For titles of exhibitions, conferences, and broadcast programs, see *9.2: Names of organizations*.

10.1.1 Italics vs. quotation marks

The general rule is similar for writings and musical works: The largest unit is italicized, the smaller unit is in quotes:

> "Song of myself" from *Leaves of grass*
>
> "Der Leiermann" from *Die Winterreise*

Major works that are part of a set are still italicized:

> *Das Rheingold* introduces the central object of *Der Ring des Nibelungen*.
>
> They attended an all-night performance of the *Anoman duta* episode from the *Ramayana*

Like articles in periodicals and essays in collections, individual parts of a larger work are in quotes, even if the larger unit is not named:

> Even the local barber whistled "La donna è mobile".

Smaller works that stand alone, including traditional songs and dance tunes, are italicized.

A major work title within a title should be italicized, but single quotes are used for a secondary title within a title:

> Paul Banks's "Berlioz's 'Marche au supplice' and *Les francs-juges*: A re-examination"

When yet another level is needed, double quotes are used:

> In her paper "A response to 'Play "Mondestrunken" for me': *Pierrot lunaire* and the global marketplace" . . .

10.1.2 Translations

If your readers will recognize titles in their original languages, do not translate them. Otherwise they may be translated without italics in parentheses:

> *A kékszakállú herceg vára* (Duke Bluebeard's castle)
>
> *Pikovaja dama* (Queen of spades)

If you follow a title with both a translation and publication information, separate the two with a semicolon and a phrase like "published in":

> *Muzika i pjevanje u Isusovačkom Kolegiju i gimnaziji u Požegi* (Music and singing in Isusovački Kolegij in Požega; published in *Sveta Cecilija*, 1936)

10.1.3 Exceptions

Some very old writings (medieval and earlier) that may not have had true titles or are known by text incipit may be given in their most familiar form:

> Aristotle's *Metaphysics*
>
> Augustine's *De musica*
>
> the *Letter to the Hebrews*

10.2 Generic titles

Generic titles are treated as descriptions, not names. They are given in English, in roman, and may be rendered variously. Some Western religious genres are capitalized. Some post–19th-century titles that use generic terms should be considered true titles; some earlier works also use them as parts of true titles.

études	Requiem
Mass	sonata no. 32, op. 111
Passion	symphony no. 4
preludes	third quartet

but

Schumann's *Requiem für Mignon*

Stravinsky's *Symphony in C*

The exception to this rule is the Renaissance cantus firmus Mass section or cycle. The genre comes first, capitalized and italicized, followed by the identifying name of the Mass, italicized and with the first letter capitalized:

Missa Osculetur me

When the identifying name is the name of the cantus firmus (chant or secular tune), put it in quotes:

Missa "L'homme armé"

When the identifying name is a description of the cantus firmus or of the Mass itself, leave out the quotes, but capitalize the first word of the identifier anyway:

Missa La sol fa re mi

Missa Sine nomine

Missa de Beata Virgine

The generic part of specified generic works is not capitalized:

Diabelli variations

Goldberg variations

10.3 Opus and catalogue numbers

The opus or catalogue number may be included the first time a work is mentioned. Numbers following *op.* and *no.* are always arabic figures;

catalogue numbers are varied. Opus or catalogue numbers are not commonly given for operas and other stage works.

> Poulenc's *Poèmes de Ronsard*, op. 38
>
> Beethoven's symphony no. 5, op. 67
>
> Haydn's D-major keyboard sonata Hob.XVI:42

Commas are used to set off supplementary information; commas are not used for necessary information. Haydn wrote more than one D-major keyboard sonata, so the catalogue number is a necessary qualifier:

> *Gelobet seist du, Jesu Christ,* BWV 91, was written for Christmas.
>
> Bach's cantata BWV 91 was written for Christmas.
>
> The Brahms C-minor piano quartet, op. 60, is an example.
>
> Brahms's piano quartet op. 60 is an example.

When a work is cited using both opus and number numbers, the *no.* component is always set off on both sides with commas:

> The sonata op. 31, no. 2, has been called the "Tempest" sonata.

10.4 Nicknames of works

A nickname is a title that was appended to a work by someone other than the composer. If it is used, put it in parentheses and quotation marks:

> Beethoven's third symphony ("Eroica")

10.5 Portions of works

References to movements by tempo or character indication are lowercase and italic:

> The *allegro con moto* movement

True titles of movements are roman and in quotes:

> "La vallée des cloches" from *Miroirs*

Small, untitled portions of works may be designated with generic terms if they are unambiguous. Portions designated by performance indications are in italics.

> In the recapitulation, the theme is transformed.

An extended stretto section follows.

The *cantabile* passage introduces a contrasting texture.

Measure numbers may be used for smaller portions of works. For works without bar lines, other designations may be used as appropriate.

The theme reappears in measures 5 through 10 of the passacaglia.

The sixth cell introduces the first sustained tone.

10.6 Manuscripts

The given titles of manuscripts are descriptive, so they may be translated (e.g., Trent codices); however, if they are in Latin, leave them in Latin.

10.6.1 RISM sigla

RISM stands for Répertoire International des Sources Musicales, one of four bibliographic projects in music sponsored by the International Musicological Society and the International Association of Music Libraries, Archives, and Documentation Centres. These projects are sometimes known as the four Rs; the others are RILM, RIPM (Répertoire International de la Presse Musicale/Retrospective Index to Music Periodicals), and RIdIM (Répertoire International d'Iconographie Musicale).

RISM is a catalogue of musical sources. Each source location has an assigned RISM siglum that indicates the country, city, and library. For example, the siglum for a manuscript in the Vatican library includes *I* for Italy, *R* for Roma, and *vat* for Biblioteca Apostolica Vaticana: *I-Rvat*. Notice that the letters for the geographic elements are capitalized and the library name is lowercase. When only one source location exists in a town, the siglum is composed of the elements for country and town only. The italicized siglum is followed by one space, the capital letters MS (without periods) when appropriate, another space, and the shelf number, which indicates the location of the manuscript in that particular library. Individual elements of the shelf number are separated by periods, without spaces. Capitalization of elements follows the library's practice.

Transcriptions of two-part polyphonic works with Latin texts from *F-Pn* MSS lat.1139, lat.3549, and lat.3719; *F-CHRm* MS 109; *E-Mn* MS 289; and *D-Mu* MS 156 are included.

Reliable reference works for searching out sigla include *Die Musik in Geschichte und Gegenwart: Personenteil* vol. 1, the *New Grove* "Sources" article, and the book *RISM-Bibliothekssigel* (München: Henle; Kassel, New York: Bärenreiter, 1999). The latter is the only source containing the complete list.

Works published in collections during the 16th and 17th centuries are listed in RISM's series B/I/1: *Recueils imprimés XVIe–XVIIe siècles* by François Lesure (München: Henle, 1960). The number for each collection comprises the four-digit year of publication and the superscripted number of the edition in that year:

> *Dolci affetti madrigali a cinque voci de diversi eccellenti musici di Roma* (RISM 1582^4)

Editions printed between 1600 and 1800 (catalogued in the RISM series A/1) have their own RISM numbers, comprising the uppercase initial of the composer's last name followed by a number, without a space:

> Giovanni Giornovichi, *Concerto a violino principale* (RISM G2382)

For copies of editions included in subsequent RISM addenda and corrigenda, the composer's initial is doubled:

> (RISM GG2382)

Whenever possible, use the RISM siglum and number when mentioning a manuscript. If no shelf number is available, spell out the full name of the library and omit the siglum. Use of the library name and the siglum together would be redundant.

10.7 Visual art

Before the mid-19th century, titles of works of visual art were usually generic and given ex post facto; they were rarely assigned by the artist. They are italicized when they refer to specific works, and they are customarily given in the language of the country where they are held:

> Lippi's *Annunciation* in the Frick Collection . . .

Generic references are not italicized, and are given in English, capitalized:

> It is not a typical 15th-century Annunciation . . .

True titles are italicized and given in the original language. If your readers are not likely to recognize the original-language title it may be translated in parentheses.

Les demoiselles d'Avignon   *Skrik* (The scream)

10.8 Online publications

Online publications are treated as collections: The title of the main page (e.g., an online journal's home page) is in italics, and secondary pages are treated as articles, with titles in quotation marks. If there is only one page, its title is italicized. If there is no true title, a descriptive phrase may be used:

Posting on Glass Onion list, 16 June 2005

References to online sources should include all components of the uniform resource locator (URL). A URL should never be capitalized, so avoid starting a sentence with one.

The history of *Musical traditions*, which evolved from a printed magazine to an online one, can be found at http://www.mustrad .org.uk/about.htm.

Line breaks may be made after a double or single slash, a colon, or the symbol @, or before most other punctuation or symbols (a break may be made on either side of an ampersand or equals sign). Hyphens should never be added to indicate line breaks, and a hyphen that is part of a URL should never appear at the end of a line.

11. NOMENCLATURE

11.1 Pitches

Pitch names given without regard to specific octaves are uppercase and roman:

symphony in A   the opening D–A dyad

Accidentals follow the pitch name, without a space:

The third symphony, which is in E♭ major . . .

References to specific pitches should be standardized according to one of the three most widely used systems: the Helmholtz system, the system used by organists (use this only for specialized writings for organists), or the standard recommended by the Acoustical Society of America. For the latter, which is our preference, the pitch class is symbolized by a capitalized roman letter, followed without a space by an arabic number indicating the relevant octave. An octave number refers to pitches from a given C through the B one major seventh above it. Any B♯ gets the same octave number as the B just below it; thus B♯3 is enharmonically C4. Likewise, any C♭ gets the same octave number as the C just above it; C♭4 is the same as B3.

Helmholtz	organ	ASA	
C_1	CCC	C1	
C	CC	C2	cello C
c	C	C3	viola C
c'	c	C4	middle C
c"	c'	C5	soprano C
c'''	c"	C6	Queen of the Night C
c''''	c'''	C7	

11.2 Chord, key, and scale denotations

Arabic numbers in chord denotations should be superscript:

V^7 I^6

Descriptive names for chords, keys, and scales are not capitalized:

F-major triad   pentatonic scale

sonata in C minor   diminished-seventh chord

However, the use or nonuse of capitals to differentiate them in abbreviations (e.g., DM for D major, Dm for D minor) can be useful for certain kinds of annotation.

11.3 Modal systems

In writings on melody, *mode* has two overlapping but distinct meanings: *scale* and *melodic type*. The former denotes a sequence of pitches in which one pitch is considered fundamental; the latter indicates more detail, such as characteristic motives or phrases. Writings about mode in Western music in the Middle Ages and Renaissance tend to discuss melodic types, while writings on jazz, traditional, or non-Western musics tend to use *mode* or modal terminology to refer to scales. In some ethnomusicological writings *mode* is used as a generic designation for non-Western melodic types.

Mode also has a specific meaning in reference to medieval Western rhythmic practices.

11.3.1 Western melodic modes

These are generally referred to as "the church modes". Since their names are derived from proper nouns, they are capitalized, unlike the designations *major* and *minor*.

Dorian mode   Phrygian cadence

11.3.2 Non-Western melodic and rhythmic types

While the word *mode* may be used to refer to these, the indigenous terms are preferred. Most systems that have terms for melodic types have separate terms for scales.

The generic names for melodic and rhythmic types are treated like other generic names: They are lowercase and roman.

maqām   tāla

rāga   usul

Specific instances are treated as unassimilated terms: They are lowercase and italic.

rāga pūrvikalyāṇī   *maqām ḥijāz*

11.3.2.1 Distinct traditions

Do not conflate distinct regional traditions by standardizing their names.

Maqām is the general Arabic term, but *makam* (Turkey), *muğam* (Azerbaijan), and *muqam* (Uyghur people) denote separate traditions.

The Karnatak terms *raga* and *tala* are considered to be assimilated by standard English dictionaries, and may therefore appear without diacritics; however, the diacritics are retained in ethnomusicological writings. These terms are often used in general discussions of Indian music; in discussions of Hindustani music alone, the northern versions, *rāg* and *tāl*, are used. When these terms are components of more specific ones, the appropriate regional forms are retained (e.g., the Hindustani *rāg jaunpurī* and *tīntāl*, the Karnatak *rāga bēgaḍa* and *ādi tāla*).

12. FOREIGN LANGUAGES

For non-English names of persons, places, and organizations, see *9: Names*. See also *4.1: Non-Western plurals*; *7.1: Terms*; *11.3.2: Non-Western melodic and rhythmic types*.

12.1 Special characters

Many word processing programs now provide letters with various diacritics in a "symbol" or "special characters" menu, and some allow for ways of entering them with key combinations. Diacritics should never be omitted; to do so is to misspell the word.

12.1.1 The scharfes s (ß)

German has rules regarding use of *ß* vs. *ss*, so care must be taken in adding or removing *ß*. There is no uppercase version of the character, so if a word with *ß* must be rendered entirely in capital letters the *ß* must be changed to *SS*.

The Waltz King used the *ß*; the composer of *Elektra* did not.

12.2 Capitalization

Many languages do not capitalize adjectives derived from proper nouns as English does: our *German* is their *deutsch*, *allemand*, etc.; our *Mozartean* is their *mozartisch*, *mozartien*, etc.

Unassimilated German nouns are capitalized; assimilated ones are not (see *8.3: Assimilated German nouns*).

Many European languages capitalize only the first words of the names of institutions. In this instance consistency overrides the wish to honor the practices of other languages. Even in a foreign language, the name of an institution is capitalized throughout.

12.3 Transliteration

Thanks to the International Organization for Standardization (ISO), efforts at transliteration need no longer be plagued by parochialism and inconsistency. Now that the ISO has established standards for transliterating non-Latin writing systems into Latin characters, there is no reason to resort to improvised or anachronistic solutions.

12.3.1 Cyrillic characters

The case for standardized transliteration of languages written in Cyrillic characters, such as Russian, is particularly strong in the context of practices in other Slavic languages. The interface of Serbian and Croatian provides a compelling touchstone: The two are very close linguistically, but Serbian uses Cyrillic characters while Croatian represents the same sounds in corresponding Latin characters. To readers of Croatian and other Slavic languages that use Latin characters, *Tchaikovsky* looks simply inaccurate, or at least eccentric; *Čajkovskij* looks perfectly natural.

Old attachments can be tenacious, and some music reference works that otherwise embrace ISO standards still cling to the old, familiar ways of transliterating famous names. However, publications that serve a more international readership, such as *Die Musik in Geschichte und Gegenwart* and *RILM abstracts of music literature*, view transliteration in a larger context. We have our "Stravinsky rule" for émigrés who customarily published under a particular version of their names, but otherwise we believe that a consistent international perspective is increasingly appropriate.

Table 1 may be used for transliterating Cyrillic characters; tables for other languages are available from the ISO.

Russian	Latin	pronunciation
А а	A a	ah
Б б	B b	
В в	V v	
Г г	G g	
Д д	D d	
Е е	E e	yeh
Ё ё	Ë ë	yo
Ж ж	Ž ž	zh
З з	Z z	
И и	I i	eee (long)
Й й	J j	ee (short)
К к	K k	
Л л	L l	
М м	M m	
Н н	N n	
О о	O o	oh
П п	P p	
Р р	R r	
С с	S s	
Т т	T t	
У у	U u	oo (as in "too")
Ф ф	F f	
Х х	H h	kh (as in German "ach")
Ц ц	C c	ts
Ч ч	Č č	ch
Ш ш	Š š	sh
Щ щ	Šč šč	shch
ъ	'	"hard sign" (obsolete; for transliteration of historical titles or names)
ы	Y y	"hard e" (a vowel not found in English)
ь	'	"soft sign" (softens the consonant preceding it)
Э э	Ė ė	eh
Ю ю	ju	yoo
Я я	ja	yah

Table 1: Cyrillic transliteration

12.3.2 Chinese

12.3.2.1 Mandarin

Chinese is a family of mutually unintelligible spoken languages, all represented by a single ideographic writing system; each character has different pronunciations in different languages. Mandarin, a fully standardized language based on the dialects radiating out of the Yellow River valley, is the official spoken language throughout the Chinese-speaking world, so Chinese words are usually transliterated in the Mandarin pronunciation. No attempt is currently made to represent syllabic tone.

Two romanization systems for Mandarin are in wide international use: the older Wade-Giles system and the newer Hanyu Pinyin. The latter is now almost universally used except in Taiwan, where it has had negative political connotations; but Pinyin is increasingly common in Taiwan, even in some official uses such as Taipei street signs. In any case, Wade-Giles has no more official status there than Pinyin does.

Hanyu Pinyin should be used as a general rule, with some exceptions noted below. You can learn to differentiate the two on sight: Wade-Giles by its apostrophes after initial consonants, syllables ending in *h*, frequent use of *ê* and *ü*, and hyphens between syllables; Hanyu Pinyin by its use of *b, d, g, j, r, z, c, q, x*, the absence of final *h* and of *ê* (*ü* does occur, but not as frequently), and the closing up of words in which Wade-Giles uses hyphens.

Translation	Wade-Giles	Hanyu-Pinyin
hammer dulcimer	yang-ch'in	yangqin
Shandong opera	Lü-chü	lüju
Cantonese opera	Yüeh-chü	yueju
China	Chung-kuo	Zhongguo
Canton (province)	Kuang-tung	Guangdong
[personal name]	Mao Tse-tung	Mao Zedong
[personal name]	Têng Hsiao-p'ing	Deng Xiaoping

Another frequently arising problem is that, although most library catalogues using the Latin alphabet have adopted Pinyin, many continue to treat each syllable as a separate word (with some exceptions).

Translation	Library catalogue style	ISO style
Dictionary of Chinese music	*Zhongguo yin yue ci dian*	*Zhongguo yinyue cidian*
People's Music Publisher	Ren min yin yue chu ban she	Renmin Yinyue Chubanshe

In the closed-up rather than hyphenated style, an apostrophe is used to show syllable boundaries that would otherwise be ambiguous:

Xi'an (Tang Dynasty capital) vs. xian (single syllable, many meanings)

min'ge (traditional song) vs. ming'e (quota)

A peculiarity due to the custom of not indicating tone is the use of the spelling *Shaanxi* to distinguish the name of one province (first syllable has a low-rising tone) from that of its neighbor to the east, *Shanxi* (first syllable has a high-level tone).

12.3.2.2 Dialects and non-Han languages

Chinese languages other than Mandarin are commonly called "dialects", a confusing usage since they generally have complex dialectologies of their own. Because of the vicissitudes of history and the peculiarities of the writing system, these languages have no standardized versions or official status anywhere (with a few exceptions: Cantonese in Hong Kong, and recently Holo/Fujian and Hakka in Taiwan), and no romanizations of sufficiently wide acceptance to be used consistently; nevertheless they are as real, and as culturally distinct, as Catalan or Bosnian. Of course, many peoples within the borders of China are ethnically and linguistically not Han (Chinese) at all.

For non-Mandarin place and ethnicity names, ethnolinguistic terminology, and personal names, if there is a standard English spelling it is preferred to the Hanyu Pinyin version (see also *9.1.2.5: Other considerations for particular languages*). Some examples follow.

Hong Kong should always be given its English name, never the Pinyin Xianggang. For places within Taiwan, the conventional Wade-Giles names may be retained:

T'aipei (or Taipei)   Kaohsiung

For place names from the non-Chinese regions of the north and west—Manchuria, Inner Mongolia, Xinjiang, and Tibet—Pinyin should be avoided in favor of non-Chinese names (Harbin, Hohhot, Ürümqi, etc.). Similarly, there are standard English names for some Chinese subethnicities that are preferable to the Pinyin terms (Cantonese, Shanghainese, etc.). *Szechuanese* for Sichuan is obsolete except on restaurant menus; *Pekingese* is only for the dog breed, otherwise always use Beijing with no suffix.

Pinyin should never be used for names and terms from languages used in China by people with independent literacy traditions, such as Tibetan, Uyghur, Mongolian, and Manchu. Other minority groups such as Naxi, Xibo, Miao, and Yao use spellings developed by Chinese linguists and ethnographers based on Pinyin principles, and these should be adopted.

In a discussion of local culture, the use of terms transliterated from the spoken languages of Guangdong, Fujian, Shanghai, and so on is desirable. While such terms will generally have Mandarin (Pinyin) equivalents, these are not felt by native speakers to have the flavor of the local term, and sometimes are directly in conflict with it. For example, the short melodies that are the basis of extended pieces in *yueju* (Cantonese opera) are known in Cantonese as *siu kuk*. The exactly corresponding Mandarin *xiaoqu* has been used to refer to an instrumental genre, and to popular urban song in Hubei province.

It is possible to use a term in both languages:

The hammer dulcimer is called *yeungkam* in Cantonese (*yangqin* in Mandarin).

13. QUOTATIONS

13.1 When to quote

Overuse of quotation is tempting for some academic writers: Lacking a verbal flair of their own, they seek to borrow it from others. On the other hand, an otherwise drab survey of the literature on a particular topic may be enlivened by the inclusion of different voices, particularly ones with a distinctive sound. To some extent, decisions on whether to quote or to paraphrase should be based on the ultimate clarity and readability of the passage. A reader becomes impatient with long, unnecessary quotes that could have been neatly summarized; but the exact words of an author with whom you are arguing, or who supports your argument, may be vital to your purpose.

13.2 Quotation vs. plagiarism

With few exceptions (see *16.1: When to cite sources*), phrases and sentences that are not your own must be cited. The doctrine of fair use allows quotation of small amounts of verbal, visual, or musical material for illustration, comparison, or criticism, as long as the original sources are clearly documented (see *16: Citations*). Quotation without documentation is plagiarism. If you wish to include more than a relatively small amount of copyrighted material—most or all of a poem, for example—in writing that will be published, permission must be granted by the copyright holder.

Copyright law has many gray areas, and it varies in different places and situations. When in doubt, check with a qualified lawyer.

13.3 Introducing changes

The wording of quotations must never be changed, although ellipsis points may be used to omit unnecessary words. Three periods with spaces before, between, and after (. . .) indicate omitted material; four periods with no space before indicate the end of a sentence (the first period) followed by omitted material. Care should be taken that the omission does not change the meaning or produce a grammatically or syntactically incorrect passage.

> She summed up her critique: "This type of analysis creates an impression of esoteric insight. . . . But . . . does it really illuminate anything beyond itself?"

Other than ellipsis points, the only changes that may be introduced are small matters of punctuation (e.g., a final period may be omitted as necessary), letter case (e.g., an initial letter may be changed from lowercase to capital), addition or deletion of end- or footnotes, and—where absolutely necessary—a word may be replaced or explained by a bracketed addition:

> He replied that the composer in question "was not fit to shine [Mozart's] shoes".

13.4 Placement

13.4.1 Block quotations

Longer quotations are set off from the text in blocks. These may be indented or they may use a smaller font size—or both—but they always begin on a new line, after a blank line. Opinions differ as to how long a quote must be in order to be set off; generally, blocks should not comprise just a few lines or a single sentence.

13.4.2 Run-in quotations

Briefer quotations are not set off in blocks; if they do not comprise full sentences, the text around them is phrased so that the resulting sentences are syntactically correct. The minor admissible changes noted above may be employed.

14. ILLUSTRATIONS

Tables, figures, and musical examples are separately numbered (even if there is only one) and so designated. When referring to them in a sentence, spell out the word; if the reference is parenthetical, it is abbreviated.

Table 1 lists the yearly wages of each court musician.

The album cover (fig. 3) depicts happy natives in festive costumes.

The theme is unornamented at first (ex. 7).

14.1 Musical examples

If these are inserted in the text, limit them to what is absolutely necessary for understanding the points you wish to make. Examples from ensemble works should be presented in reductions whenever possible. Full ethnomusicological transcriptions may be included in an appendix, but they should not interrupt the text unless they are relatively brief.

Captions should identify the example succinctly, repeating information found in the text only when necessary to avoid confusion. If complete works or transcriptions are presented, the caption should contain full titles and the full names of composers, informants, or sources.

Ex. 1. Anton Webern, "Erlösung" from *Drei Lieder*, op. 18, mm. 1–3.

Ex. 2. *Barbara Allen*, sung by Fleecy Fox (recorded by John Quincy Wolf, Jr., 1963)

Ex. 3. *Virtutem titulos/vestreque glorie* from *I-La* MS 247, n. 3.

14.2 Tables and figures

As with musical examples, limit in-text tables, diagrams, and figures to relatively small ones, and save large ones for an appendix. In general, captions should simply identify them without unnecessarily repeating information found in the text. However, if the figure is a reproduction of an artwork it should be treated as a complete work and captioned accordingly. If the artwork is the object of an iconographic study, include date, medium, dimensions, location, and inventory number if possible.

Table 1. Court musicians' wages, 1745.

Fig. 5. Fleecy Fox at home, 1963.

Fig. 6. Pablo Picasso, *Guitar, sheet music, and wine glass*. Detail.

Fig. 1. "Egy Magyar verbunkos: Dudás", Hungarian bagpiper with
three soldiers dancing verbunkos (Vienna, ca. 1840).
Watercolored engraving, 214 x 285 mm. Private collection.

15. ABSTRACT WRITING

15.1 Content

An abstract ought to convey every important aspect of the writing it describes. Nonessential matters should be omitted, so as not to mislead the reader. Do not spend too much time describing the item's intellectual background; it is more important to deal with its content. If you are presenting new findings, concentrate on them and do not rehearse the known facts. State clearly the main conclusion or conclusions given in the item being abstracted (although not all research yields specific conclusions).

Providing concrete information such as personal names, places, and names of organizations is always a desideratum as long as the item gives substantial information about them (see *9: Names*). If you are referring to a manuscript, give its present location (institution and complete shelf number; see *10.6.1: RISM sigla*). If you are referring to specific musical or scholarly works, give their full titles (see *10: Titles*). If you are referring to one or more elements of a work, indicate where they are found in the longer work (e.g., for a song from a cycle, name the cycle as well as the song; for an étude in a set of études, name or number the set and give the number of the étude). Indicate the time period under discussion as precisely as possible. If you use unusual terms, define them. If you are dealing with pedagogy, indicate the level of education concerned.

15.2 Style

Avoid colloquial or informal language and write in complete sentences. Do not include personal views on the value of the item being abstracted. Many effective abstracts resemble a single well-shaped paragraph, with topic sentence, development, and conclusion. Writing in the voice of the author (declaratively) yields a more vivid abstract than does describing the author's work, and lends itself to specificity.

Here is a pair of examples of abstracts for "Music iconography in Panselli's *Coro*", an article in an exhibition catalogue. (These and the following examples describe fictitious publications.)

> (1) Supports the attribution to Allendro, first proposed by Ridgeway, of the music in Panselli's *Coro d'angeli*, and suggests that Guido Sforza may have been responsible for the collaboration between composer and artist. The music's iconographic significance

is examined. A new reconstruction of it as a canon, rising a whole tone at each repetition, is proposed. It is argued that this canonic design originated with Allendro.

(2) The musical inscription in Michelangelo Panselli's *Coro d'angeli*, drawn on a book held by an angel, is by Sandro Allendro, as proposed by Millicent Ridgeway. Guido Sforza may have arranged a collaboration on the painting, bringing together the composer and painter. The text of Allendro's piece relates to the iconographic design as a whole, completing an allegorical portrait of the Sforzas as ideal human beings. A new reconstruction of the music as a canon, which rises a whole tone at each repetition, suggests that the musical work's design was the painter's.

The first of these is descriptive, the second declarative. In theory, one can include the same information with either approach, but in practice, the declarative style forces a writer to be more specific. (Where the descriptive version says "the music's iconographic significance is examined," the declarative version says: "The text of Allendro's piece relates to the iconographic design as a whole, completing an allegorical portrait of the Sforzas as ideal human beings.") Further, the descriptive style normally involves the writer in a series of passive constructions, as in the last three sentences of the first example.

Note that the second abstract used complete personal names, which is correct, since none of the people mentioned here is famous enough for instant recognition.

15.2.1 Further examples

Each of the following examples comprises an abstract with a number of lapses in style, followed by the same abstract with improvements.

EXAMPLE 1: "Schütz revisited", an article.

> The author attempts a complete reevaluation of Schütz's position in musical history through an examination of all known contemporary biographical and musical sources, resulting in a considerable change in our understanding of this composer.

This descriptive abstract leaves a number of questions in the reader's mind. What is Schütz's historical position? What method was used to accomplish a reevaluation? Are there any dates, personal names, or names of organizations involved? What conclusion was reached? The following declarative abstract, though not much longer, answers these questions.

> Recent findings in Schütz's biography and on the sources of his music suggest fundamental revisions in our assessment of his personality and artistic profile. In particular, the repertorial emphases set by the German Singbewegung of the 1920s—which still shape the selection of his music most frequently encountered—appear to represent not the core of his creative achievement but the periphery.

EXAMPLE 2: "Recordings in the singing room", an article.

> Proposes a methodology of modern singing.

The source document obviously presents a conclusion: It proposes a new method. The abstract should say what the methodology is.

> Recording technology should be used to supplement the traditional private voice lesson, allowing outstanding singers to offer a variety of permanent—if one-sided—master classes to an unlimited number of interested students.

EXAMPLE 3: *Schumann at work*, a book.

> A critical review of Schumann's method of composing melodies. Schumann's habits of composing are considered as viewed by past scholars, and in the light of new research. Comments by friends, and by Schumann himself, shed light on this question.

The author of this source document obviously had an opinion, but the abstract states neither what that opinion was, how the opinion was formed, nor what conclusions were drawn. What were Schumann's methods? How have they been viewed? Who exactly held those views? Does the book provide a new conclusion? The following abstract shows how much more useful a well-written declarative abstract can be.

> The belief widely accepted by scholars that Schumann composed only while in a kind of frenzy, or trance of inspiration, is refuted by many comments in letters and diary entries by him, and by the comments of contemporaries—the most notable admirer being Anton Gerhard Wilhelm von Alpenburg, his nephew. At least 13 remarks by Schumann between 1848 and 1850 refer to having worked hard, "though without much interest".

EXAMPLE 4: An article entitled "Peter Grossklein: Life and works" is probably, judging from the title alone, a general discussion of the composer. The following abstract correctly focuses on the major point of the general discussion, but the writing is not concise and fails to use the author's voice.

> After a general discussion of Grossklein's works, the author attempts to provide a rationale that encompasses the fact that his work took into account musical thought in the context of the philosophical thinking of the symbolist school.

Once again, a declarative abstract with simpler language is better.

> Grossklein's works show his deep interest in the musical philosophy of the symbolists.

EXAMPLE 5: "Gluck on stage", an article.

> The author suggests that, to understand the dramatic recitative in works by Gluck, a sound knowledge of the vocal techniques of the actors and vocalists of the 18th century is required on the part of listeners.

(1) The source document contains a conclusion—that listeners should be knowledgeable—so a declarative abstract is required; (2) the passive voice should be changed to the active voice; and (3) "sound knowledge" and "on the part of" are unnecessarily wordy.

> Understanding Gluck's dramatic recitative requires knowledge of the techniques of 18th-century actors and singers.

EXAMPLE 6: "A scribal tradition discovered", an article.

> The author compares manuscript psalters from the 14th to the 16th centuries preserved in church archives.

For a scholarly article, the above abstract is too vague. Factual details are required, in addition to a clear presentation of the author's conclusions: the abstract states "the author compares", but what are the results? The following declarative abstract clarifies and summarizes. Note the inclusion of RISM library sigla with shelf numbers.

> The St. Kevin Psalter (*E-Dpc* MS Kev.1234), the Steinhertz Psalters (*D-KNd* MS 9876), and all of the psalters in the collection of the Ávila Cathedral (*E-Ac* MSS 12, 34, 35, 36, 37, 453, 1120, 2231)

show emendations in many hands, apparently added over long periods. Psalters from Eastern European sources (*CZ-Psj* MS 3456,
56788, and 56798–01; *H-EGb* ins. 4564–87) show emendations by
a succession of apparently official scribes. Study of the emendations reveals a close relationship among all of these psalters, and
variant readings have provided evidence with which to construct a
tentative stemma.

EXAMPLE 7: "Music of the Central African pygmies", an article.

Music and dance are very important in pygmy culture. Turnbull's
recordings of the pygmies were all songs. The UNESCO recordings of pygmies also include flutes. Like their society, their songs
have no particular form.

The first sentence may be true, but it is true of so many cultures that it is
nearly meaningless; that importance is discussed in the article, not simply stated as it is here. We need to know who Turnbull was, and when his
recordings were made. *Song* should not be used generically for vocal music (many of Turnbull's recordings are of polyphonic group singing).
Also, *pygmy* is a very broad term; always prefer the term a particular
group uses for themselves. Ethnomusicological recordings should be
designated by the person(s) who made them, not the organization that issued them. Indigenous instrumental terms are favored over generic ones
like *flute*, though the latter may be used descriptively. The last sentence
sounds condescending, mistaking open or flexible forms for formless-
ness—an inapplicable Western concept. The following abstract ad-
dresses these concerns, and conveys much more information in not much
more space.

The function of music and dance in pygmy society is assessed, and
parallels are drawn between musical and social structures. Colin
Turnbull's recordings of the mButi people, made in the 1950s, present only vocal performances; Simha Arom's recordings of the
Benzele people from the 1960s also include performances on the
hindewhu, a one-tone pipe.

15.3 Checklist for abstractors

All abstracts should supply:

- First names of all authors, translators, collaborators, and subjects, except for very well-known persons.

- Complete titles of musical works in the original language, with index or opus numbers in their correct form. (Give original-language titles for works only when the work has a given title, however; see *10.2: Generic titles.*)

- Complete names of all associations, societies, performing groups, religious bodies, and academic and government institutions in the language of their country.

- For manuscripts, location and shelf number, with RISM siglum for the library.

- Definitions of terms not in standard music reference works.

- Complete and correct place names in their appropriate historical form. Add current forms in parentheses when referring to an earlier time; e.g., Pressburg (now Bratislava).

- Basic bibliographic information (place and date of publication) for publications referred to.

15.4 Submitting an abstract to RILM

RILM's national committees provide thousands of citations and abstracts every year, but they still might not discover all of your published work. Even if they do, they cannot always provide abstracts as detailed and accurate as the ones you can write. By far the best way to have your work represented in RILM is for you to send citations and abstracts yourself; this is easily done online at http://www.rilm.org/submit.html. RILM is happy to replace inferior abstracts with authors' submissions for writings; the new abstract will appear online within a few months.

16. CITATIONS

16.1 When to cite sources

Do not cite sources for facts that are commonly known or that comprise brief, standardized information, such as a person's name or birth and death dates. Well-known expressions do not require citation, nor do famous quotations.

> Mozart's sister Maria Anna ("Nannerl", 1751–1829) was also a talented musician.
>
> He knew very well that misery loves company.
>
> As Shakespeare noted, "all that glisters is not gold".

16.2 Citing publishers

Do not change, translate, or abridge a publisher's name. There are a few exceptions: An initial *The* and abbreviations such as *Co.*, *Ltd.*, and *Inc.* may be omitted. *Publishers*, *Publishing*, and their counterparts in other languages may also be omitted; *Books*, *Press*, and their equivalents in other languages should stay.

Publishers are capitalized in headline style (see *8.1: When to capitalize*).

> Basic Books
>
> Kasturi & Sons (for Kasturi & Sons Ltd.)
>
> Leo S. Olschki Editore (**not** Olschki)
>
> Mkuki na Nyota (for Mkuki na Nyota Publishers)
>
> University of Chicago Press (for The University of Chicago Press)

16.2.1 City names

For languages using the Latin alphabet, provide the version of the city name given in the publication itself: Do not translate it into the English version, even if you would do so in prose (see *9.3.5: A partial list of cities with alternate names*). For languages using other alphabets, use the ISO standard transliteration (see *12.3: Transliteration*).

The obvious objection to not standardizing city names in this context is that of consistency: The same bibliography may list books published in Petrograd, Leningrad, and Sankt-Peterburg, which are different historical names for the same city. In documentation, favoring one of these place names over the others is tantamount to rewriting history, a practice well beyond the domain of bibliography. It is best to treat all instances the same way, retaining whatever place name the publisher used.

There is one exception: If a publisher has chosen to render its city name in a foreign language, it may be changed to the current official name (e.g., *Nueva York* becomes *New York*).

16.2.1.1 Multiple cities

When a publisher publishes in more than one city, the cities are separated with semicolons:

> University Park; London: Pennsylvania State University Press

16.2.1.2 States, provinces, and countries

Include a state, province, or country with a publisher's city when such information is necessary. For example, if a publisher is based in Cambridge, Massachusetts, indicate *Cambridge, Mass.* to differentiate the city from Cambridge, England (which would be rendered as *Cambridge, U.K.*). Note that the standard state abbreviation (*Mass.*) is used, not the postal abbreviation (*MA*). You may also include such information for small or little-known towns, as a courtesy to the reader.

16.3 Style choice

Scholarly authors must choose between two citation styles: numbered notes (footnotes or endnotes) and in-text citations (the author-date system). In general, the former is preferred in the humanities, while the latter is preferred in the social sciences. The notes system is generally the standard for Western musicology, while the in-text system is generally the standard for ethnomusicology.

Examples of citations for several publication types are given separately below for each system in *16.4: Numbered notes and bibliographic formats* and *16.5: In-text citations and bibliographic formats*. Relevant explanatory material is repeated for each system, so readers may consult only the sections on the system required for their work.

16.4 Numbered notes and bibliographic formats

These are indicated by a superscript number at the appropriate point in the text; often this will be at the end of a quotation or paraphrase. The notes may appear either at the bottom of the same page (footnotes) or at the end of the article, chapter, section, dissertation, or book (endnotes). (The use of notes for discursive matter is discussed in *2.12.1: Parenthetical sentences.*)

Throughout this section, most of the examples of numbered notes are given in pairs: the long form used when no bibliography is supplied, and the short form used in conjunction with a bibliography.

16.4.1 Printed materials

16.4.1.1 Books

In the absence of a bibliography, all publication information is given in the first reference:

[1] Bruno Nettl, *Encounters in ethnomusicology: A memoir* (Warren, Mich.: Harmonie Park Press, 2002) 125.

Note that the author's name is not inverted, since alphabetization is not an issue.

If a bibliography is included, the first reference provides only the author's last name, the title (without subtitle), and the page number(s):

[1] Nettl, *Encounters in ethnomusicology*, 125.

In both cases, subsequent references use a shortened form of the title, often just the first word:

[8] Nettl, *Encounters*, 57–58.

Ibid. may be used for the work cited in the immediately preceding note:

[1] Nettl, *Encounters in ethnomusicology*, 125.

[2] Ibid., 126–27.

The cumbersome and potentially misleading *op. cit.* and *loc. cit.* are eschewed.

The book is entered in the bibliography thus:

> Nettl, Bruno. *Encounters in ethnomusicology: A memoir* (Warren, Mich.: Harmonie Park Press, 2002).

In some situations you may wish to give additional information:

> Lassiter, Luke E. *The power of Kiowa song: A collaborative ethnography* (Tucson: University of Arizona Press, 1998) xv, 266 p. ISBN 0-8165-1835-1. Illus., port., bibliog., index, tables, diagr., maps.

When multiple works by an author are listed in a bibliography, the author's name is replaced by five underscores after the first listing:

> Nettl, Bruno. *Encounters in ethnomusicology: A memoir* (Warren, Mich.: Harmonie Park Press, 2002).
>
> _____. *Heartland excursions: Ethnomusicological reflections on schools of music* (Urbana: University of Illinois Press, 1995).

Note that works by the same author are arranged alphabetically by title, not chronologically.

Translations and editions other than the first are indicated thus:

> Touma, Habib Hassan. *The music of the Arabs*. Trans. by Laurie Schwartz (Rev. ed.; Portland, Ore.: Amadeus, 1996).

Some books are issued simultaneously by two publishers:

> Reichling, Alfred, ed. *Orgel*. MGG prisma; Veröffentlichung der Gesellschaft der Orgelfreunde 181 (Kassel: Bärenreiter; Stuttgart: Metzler, 2001).

Note that the series information (two series, in this case) is given after the title.

16.4.1.2 Theses and dissertations

The practice of treating dissertations and theses as writings that do not merit the same treatment as published ones is gratuitously demeaning. Especially now that anyone with a computer and a printer can be a print publisher and anyone with Internet access can be an online publisher, the fact that a piece of writing has been published should not confer more status than the fact that an extended study has been accepted by a committee of recognized experts on its subject. Dissertations and theses exist in the same form as print publications—as books—and copies may be found at the granting institutions and, not infrequently, at other libraries. Titles should be italicized, and the designation *unpublished* should be omitted. Degree-granting institutions are treated similarly to publishers.

[1] Mikaela Ceridwen Griffiths, *A profile of needs: Music therapy with HIV infected children in a South African institution* (M.Mus. thesis, University of Pretoria, 2003) 46.

[1] Griffiths, *A profile of needs*, 46.

[2] Szymon Paczkowski, *Nauka o afektach w mysli muzycznej I polowy XVII wieku* (Ph.D. diss., Uniwersytet Warszawski, 1996) 213–14.

[2] Paczkowski, *Nauka o afektach w mysli muzycznej I polowy XVII wieku*, 213–14.

These items are entered in the bibliography thus:

Griffiths, Mikaela Ceridwen. *A profile of needs: Music therapy with HIV infected children in a South African institution* (M.Mus. thesis, University of Pretoria, 2003).

Paczkowski, Szymon. *Nauka o afektach w mysli muzycznej I polowy XVII wieku* (Ph.D. diss., Uniwersytet Warszawski, 1996).

16.4.1.3 Items from periodicals and collections

The first pair of examples is for an essay in a collection; the second pair is for an article in a periodical:

[1] Ferenc Farkas, "Kodály és a magyar műdal", *Kodály emlékkönyv 1997*, ed. by Ferenc Bónis. Magyar zenetörténeti tanulmányok 7 (Budapest: Püski, 1997) 61.

[1] Farkas, "Kodály és a magyar műdal", 61.

[2] David Best, "Relationships: Musical and personal—Theme and variations", *International journal of music education* 22/1 (2004) 23.

[2] Best, "Relationships: Musical and personal", 23.

Note that in the first example the series information is given before the publisher. These items are entered in the bibliography thus:

Farkas, Ferenc. "Kodály és a magyar műdal", *Kodály emlékkönyv 1997*, ed. by Ferenc Bónis. Magyar zenetörténeti tanulmányok 7 (Budapest: Püski, 1997) 60–63.

Best, David. "Relationships: Musical and personal—Theme and variations", *International journal of music education* 22/1 (2004) 21–33.

Note that end punctuation following the title goes outside quotation marks: End punctuation goes inside quotation marks only when it is part of the title (see *2.11.3: End punctuation with quotation marks*). Titles that include end punctuation are not followed by a period or comma.

Neumann, Alfred E. "What, me wordy?" *Pomo review* 21/108 (1997) 23–55.

Multiple works by the same author are treated like those described in *16.4.1.1: Books*.

16.4.1.4 Reference publications and tertiary sources

Entries in reference publications and tertiary sources are seldom cited; however, in some cases they are the only available sources—for example, when nothing else has been published on a topic, or when a publication cannot be located or is in an unfamiliar language. In rare cases, a tertiary source may provide the most current or comprehensive published treatment of a topic. For online versions of such sources, see *16.4.3.2: Online publications*.

These are treated like items in a collection. If they are signed, they are entered under the author's name; if they are unsigned, they are entered under the editor's name.

[1] Ricardo Miranda-Pérez, "Herrera de la Puente, Luis", *Die Musik in Geschichte und Gegenwart: Personenteil*, ed. by Ludwig Finscher (2nd ed. rev.; Kassel: Bärenreiter; Stuttgart: Metzler, 2002) vol. 8, 1421.

[1] Miranda-Pérez, "Herrera de la Puente, Luis", 1421.

[2] Harold S. Powers, et al., "Mode", *The new Grove dictionary of music and musicians*, ed. by Stanley Sadie and John Tyrrell (2nd ed. rev.; London: Macmillan; New York: Grove's Dictionaries, 2001) vol. 16, 842.

[2] Powers, et al., "Mode", 842.

[3] Colin Larkin, ed., "Yamaguchi, Momoe", *The Guinness encyclopedia of popular music* (2nd ed.; Middlesex: Guinness; New York: Stockton, 1995) 4578.

[3] Larkin, ed., "Yamaguchi, Momoe", 4578.

These items are entered in the bibliography thus:

Miranda-Pérez, Ricardo. "Herrera de la Puente, Luis", *Die Musik in Geschichte und Gegenwart: Personenteil*, ed. by Ludwig Finscher (2nd ed. rev.; Kassel: Bärenreiter; Stuttgart: Metzler, 2002) vol. 8, 1421.

Powers, Harold S., et al. "Mode", *The new Grove dictionary of music and musicians*, ed. by Stanley Sadie (2nd ed. rev.; London: Macmillan; New York: Grove's Dictionaries, 2001) vol. 16, 775–860.

Larkin, Colin, ed. "Yamaguchi, Momoe", *The Guinness encyclopedia of popular music* (2nd ed.; Middlesex: Guinness; New York: Stockton, 1995) 4578.

Note that edition information is given in parentheses with the publisher information.

RILM abstracts in print are cited the same way as those in online sources; see *16.4.3.2: Online publications*.

16.4.1.5 Notes and commentary in scores and editions

These are treated like items in collections:

[1] Richard Strauss, "Geleitwort", *Capriccio* by Clemens Kraus and Richard Strauss (Mainz: B. Schotts; London: Boosey & Hawkes, 1942) 3.

[1] Strauss, "Geleitwort", 3.

[2] Charles Jacobs, "Critical notes", *Frescobaldi's "Il primo libro de madrigali a cinque voci"*, ed. by Charles Jacobs (University Park; London: Pennsylvania State University Press, 1983) 152.

[2] Jacobs, "Critical notes", 152.

These items are entered in the bibliography thus:

> Strauss, Richard. "Geleitwort", *Capriccio* by Clemens Kraus and Richard Strauss (Mainz: B. Schotts; London: Boosey & Hawkes, 1942) 1–4.
>
> Jacobs, Charles. "Critical notes", *Frescobaldi's "Il primo libro de madrigali a cinque voci"*, ed. by Charles Jacobs (University Park; London: Pennsylvania State University Press, 1983) 151–57.

Note that if you are citing the second example as an edition (as opposed to only citing the editor's notes) it is listed under the composer's name, not the editor's; see *16.4.1.9: Editions of music.*

16.4.1.6 Reviews

Titled reviews are treated as articles:

> [1] Alex Ross, "Resurrection: The Passion according to Osvaldo Golijov", *The New Yorker* 77/2 (5 March 2001) 101.
>
> [1] Ross, "Resurrection", 101

Untitled reviews are listed with a brief description instead of a title:

> [2] Daniel Avorgbedor, review of Charry *Mande music*, in *The world of music* 47/2 (2005) 165.
>
> [2] Avorgbedor, review of Charry *Mande music*, 165.

These items are entered in the bibliography thus:

> Ross, Alex. "Resurrection: The Passion according to Osvaldo Golijov", *The New Yorker* 77/2 (2001) 100–01.
>
> Avorgbedor, Daniel. Review of Charry *Mande music*, in *The world of music* 47/2 (2005) 163–67.

Note that for the second example the word *in* is inserted for clarity.

16.4.1.7 Liner notes

Some liner notes have titles other than the title of the recording; many do not. In either case, citations should state that they are liner notes and give basic publishing data for the recording.

[1] Tina Frühauf, "Introduction to the libretto/Introduction du livret/ Vorwort zum Libretto". Liner notes for *Charles Gounod: Faust* (Andante 3995, 2002) 54–57; 116–19; 182–86.

[1] Frühauf, "Introduction to the libretto".

[2] Nat Hentoff, liner notes for *The freewheelin' Bob Dylan* (Columbia Records CS 8786, 1963).

[2] Hentoff, liner notes for *The freewheelin' Bob Dylan*.

These are entered in the bibliography thus:

Frühauf, Tina. "Introduction to the libretto/Introduction du livret/ Vorwort zum Libretto". Liner notes for *Charles Gounod: Faust* (Andante 3995, 2002) 54–57; 116–19; 182–86.

Hentoff, Nat. Liner notes for *The freewheelin' Bob Dylan* (Columbia Records CS 8786, 1963).

Sometimes supplements, updates, or errata for liner notes may be found online; these are treated as online publications (see *16.4.3.2: Online publications*). Full publishing data for the original publication is not necessary, but the owner or sponsor of the website should be noted. The year of the online publication is given, not that of the original recording.

Yamplosky, Philip. "Liner notes supplements: What is a gamelan?". http://www.folkways.si.edu/projects_initiatives/indonesian/ liner_notes/volume14.html (Smithsonian Folkways Recordings, 1998).

For rules regarding line breaks in URLs, see *10.8: Online publications*.

16.4.1.8 Program notes

These are issued in various forms. Some, like *Stagebill*, are issued as periodicals; these are treated as such in bibliographies, and the program notes are treated like articles. Others are issued as books, with changeable details—such as lists of performers—provided as an insert; these are treated like collections of essays. For these two cases, see *16.4.1.3: Items from periodicals and collections*.

For notes in programs that are neither periodicals nor collections, titles of notes and programs are given when they appear, as is the performance date or date range. The sponsoring organization or venue may serve as the publisher. The publication may or may not be paginated.

[1] Claude Rostand, "Jean Rivier: 7ᵉ symphonie en fa". Program notes for Orchestre de Paris, 22–25 March 1972 (Paris: Société des Concerts du Conservatoire, 1972).

[1] Rostand, "Jean Rivier: 7ᵉ symphonie en fa".

[2] Adrienne Fried Block, "The Philharmonic promotes chamber music, 1843–68". Program notes for *The New York Philharmonic ensembles in a historically informed program of chamber music*, 2 December 2002 (New York: City University of New York, 2002) 1–4.

[2] Block, "The Philharmonic promotes chamber music, 1843–68".

[3] Harold Rosenthal, program notes for *Tristan und Isolde* by Richard Wagner, 3 July 1971 (London: Royal Opera House Covent Garden, 1971).

[3] Rosenthal, program notes for *Tristan und Isolde*.

These items are entered in the bibliography thus:

Rostand, Claude. "Jean Rivier: 7ᵉ symphonie en fa". Program notes for Orchestre de Paris, 22–25 March 1972 (Paris: Société des Concerts du Conservatoire, 1972).

Block, Adrienne Fried. "The Philharmonic promotes chamber music, 1843–68". Program notes for *The New York Philharmonic ensembles in a historically informed program of chamber music*, 2 December 2002 (New York: City University of New York, 2002) 1–4.

Rosenthal, Harold. Program notes for *Tristan und Isolde* by Richard Wagner, 3 July 1971 (London: Royal Opera House Covent Garden, 1971).

16.4.1.9 Editions of music

Works are not cited bibliographically or in notes unless a particular edition is discussed:

[1] Loreto Vittori, *La Galatea*. Ed. by Thomas D. Dunn (Middleton, Wis.: A-R Editions, 2002).

[1] Vittori, *La Galatea*.

Note that the composer is the author; the editor's name follows the title. The item is entered in the bibliography thus:

> Vittori, Loreto. *La Galatea*. Ed. by Thomas D. Dunn (Middleton, Wis.: A-R Editions, 2002).

For multivolume editions of complete works, series information is given after the title:

> [1] Georg Friedrich Händel, *Israel in Egypt, HWV 54*. Hallische Händel-Ausgabe: Kritische Gesamtausgabe I—Oratorien und große Kantaten 14 (Kassel: Bärenreiter; Stuttgart: Metzler, 1999).
>
> [1] Händel, *Israel in Egypt*.

The item is entered in the bibliography thus:

> Händel, Georg Friedrich. *Israel in Egypt, HWV 54*. Hallische Händel-Ausgabe: Kritische Gesamtausgabe I—Oratorien und große Kantaten 14 (Kassel: Bärenreiter; Stuttgart: Metzler, 1999).

Exceptionally, critical editions published as part of a dissertation or thesis are listed under the name of the editor/author.

> Spence, Marcia Louise. *Carl Nielsen's quintet for winds, op. 43: A critical edition* (DMA diss., University of North Texas, 1995).

For items in the volume other than the work itself, see *16.4.1.5: Notes and commentary in scores and editions*.

16.4.1.10 Technical drawings of instruments

The person who made the drawing is treated as the author. Titles are in standardized form, in English, giving the instrument type and maker (*Anonymous* when necessary), with the place and year it was made (approximate, if necessary) in parentheses. The location of the instrument is indicated, including the inventory number in the collection. The date of the drawing is given, even if it is the same as the publication date, and the number of sheets is noted.

> [1] Fer Vromans, *Barrel organ by Diederik Nicolaus Winkel (Amsterdam, ca. 1820)*. Owned by Haags Gemeentemuseum, Ea 178-X-1952. Drawn in 1988. 6 sheets ('s-Gravenhage: Haags Gemeentemuseum, 1988).
>
> [1] Fer Vromans, *Barrel organ by Diederik Nicolaus Winkel (Amsterdam, ca. 1820)*.

The item is entered in the bibliography thus:

> Vromans, Fer. *Barrel organ by Diederik Nicolaus Winkel (Amster-dam, ca. 1820)*. Owned by Haags Gemeentemuseum, Ea 178-X-1952. Drawn in 1988. 6 sheets. ('s-Gravenhage: Haags Gemeente-museum, 1988).

16.4.2 Audio and audiovisual materials

Mass-media publishers are often not associated with a single city, and the location of their executive offices may not be relevant. In such cases, do not force a place name.

16.4.2.1 Sound recordings

Recordings may be listed in a discography; they should be cited in notes only if they are discussed in the text. References may be grouped by com-poser, performer, producer, or compiler as appropriate, in short or long note forms:

> [1] Béla Bartók, *Pour les enfants*. Michel Béroff, piano. 2 LPs; in-cludes other Bartók piano works (EMI La Voix de Son Maître 2C 167-16.246/247, 1979).
>
> [1] Bartók, *Pour les enfants*.
>
> [2] Dolly Parton, *Little sparrow*. CD (Sugar Hill Records 3927, 2001).
>
> [2] Parton, *Little sparrow*.
>
> [3] Robin Broadbank and Joep Bor, prods., *The raga guide: A survey of 74 Hindustani ragas*. 4 CDs (Nimbus Records 5536–5539, 1999).
>
> [3] Broadbank and Bor, *The raga guide*.
>
> [4] Lomax, Alan, comp., *Carriacou Calaloo*. The Alan Lomax col-lection: Caribbean voyage. CD (Rounder Records 1722, 1999).
>
> [4] Lomax, *Carriacou Calaloo*.

Note that the Bartók work title is given as it appears in the publication cited; it is not changed to its original language.

These items are entered in the discography thus:

> Bartók, Béla. *Pour les enfants*. Michel Béroff, piano. 2 LPs; includes other Bartók piano works (EMI La Voix de Son Maître 2C 167-16.246/247, 1979).

> Parton, Dolly. *Little sparrow*. CD (Sugar Hill Records 3927, 2001).

> Broadbank, Robin, and Joep Bor, prods. *The raga guide: A survey of 74 Hindustani ragas*. 4 CDs (Nimbus Records 5536–5539, 1999).

> Lomax, Alan, comp. *Carriacou Calaloo*. The Alan Lomax collection: Caribbean voyage. CD (Rounder Records 1722, 1999).

There is no need to cite individual tracks in notes; specific sections, titles, etc., are supplied in the text:

> Parton has even recorded standards such as Cole Porter's "I get a kick out of you".[2]

> [2] Parton, *Little sparrow*.

For liner notes, see *16.4.1.7: Liner notes*.

16.4.2.2 Films and video recordings

Films and video recordings may be listed in a filmography or videography (the two may be combined); they should be cited in notes only if they are discussed in the text. They are treated like books, with an indication of the medium for the full citation. References may be grouped by composer, director, producer, or title as appropriate, in short or long note forms:

> [1] Giuseppe Verdi. *Nabucco*. DVD. Teatro alla Scala, Riccardo Muti, conductor (Kultur D2042, 2003).

> [1] Verdi, *Nabucco*.

> [2] Alfred Hitchcock. *Psycho*. DVD (MCA Home Video, 1998).

> [2] Hitchcock. *Psycho*.

> [3] David Evans, William Ferris, and Judy Peiser. *Gravel Springs fife and drum*. 16mm (Memphis: Center for Southern Folklore, 1971).

> [3] Evans, Ferris, and Peiser, *Gravel Springs fife and drum*.

[4] *Noreg i dans og spel.* VHS (Dragvoll: Rådet for Folkemusikk og Folkedans, 2002).

[4] *Noreg i dans og spel.*

Feature films are treated similarly to musical works: They are only cited when a specific edition is under discussion. So, for example, *Psycho* need not be cited as a publication if the reference is to Bernard Herrmann's score for the film; however, if the reference is to one of the additional features added for the DVD edition, the above citation is in order.

These items are entered in the filmography or videography thus:

Verdi, Giuseppe. *Nabucco.* DVD. Teatro alla Scala, Riccardo Muti, conductor (Kultur D2042, 2003).

Hitchcock, Alfred. *Psycho.* DVD (MCA Home Video, 1998).

Evans, David, William Ferris, and Judy Peiser. *Gravel Springs fife and drum.* 16mm (Memphis: Center for Southern Folklore, 1971).

Noreg i dans og spel. VHS (Dragvoll: Rådet for Folkemusikk og Folkedans, 2002).

16.4.2.3 Music videos

These are listed by performer in long or short forms:

[1] Selena Quintanilla Pérez, *La carcacha.* VHS (EMI Latin, 1992).

[1] Quintanilla Pérez, *La carcacha.*

[2] Outkast. *Hey ya.* DVD (La Face, 2003).

[2] Outkast, *Hey ya.*

These items are entered in the videography thus:

Quintanilla Pérez, Selena. *La carcacha.* VHS (EMI Latin, 1992).

Outkast. *Hey ya.* DVD (La Face, 2003).

Note that Selena is listed under her full name, not her stage name. When necessary, the stage name follows the full name in parentheses. See *9.1.3: Name changes, pseudonyms, and sobriquets.*

16.4.2.4 Radio and television broadcasts

Typography for titles should be slightly different than it is in prose: Treat both ongoing programs and single ones as works, and treat series as institutions (see *8.1: When to capitalize*). Like films, they may be grouped by composer, director, producer(s), or title as appropriate, in short or long note forms:

[1] Karlheinz Stockhausen, *Mittwochs-Gruß* (BBC Radio 3, 27 August 2005).

[1] Stockhausen, *Mittwochs-Gruß*.

[2] Bruno Monsaingeon, *The art of the violin* (Great Performances, PBS, 22 May 2005).

[2] Monsaingeon, *The art of the violin*.

[3] *The Ed Sullivan show* (CBS, 9 February 1964).

[3] *The Ed Sullivan show*.

These items are entered in the bibliography thus:

Stockhausen, Karlheinz. *Mittwochs-Gruß* (BBC Radio 3, 27 August 2005).

Monsaingeon, Bruno. *The art of the violin* (Great Performances, PBS, 22 May 2005).

The Ed Sullivan show (CBS, 9 February 1964).

16.4.3 Electronic publications

16.4.3.1 CD-ROMs

These are treated like books, with an indication of the medium for the full citation:

[1] Alan Rich, *Bach and before: A collector's guide to compact discs*. CD-ROM (Santa Monica: Voyager, 1992).

[1] Rich, *Bach and before*.

The item is entered in the bibliography thus:

Rich, Alan. *Bach and before: A collector's guide to compact discs*. CD-ROM (Santa Monica: Voyager, 1992).

16.4.3.2 Online publications

Online publications are not always paginated; this example from an online journal appears on a sequence of five web pages. In the long form, this information is represented by *bain3* in the URL.

> [1] Jennifer Bain, "Hildegarde on 34th Street: Chant in the marketplace", *Echo* 6/1 (2004) http://www.echo.ucla.edu/volume6-issue1/bain/bain3.html.

> [1] Bain, "Hildegarde on 34th Street", 3.

The item is entered in the bibliography thus:

> Bain, Jennifer. "Hildegarde on 34th Street: Chant in the marketplace", *Echo* 6/1 (2004) http://www.echo.ucla.edu/volume6-issue1/bain/bain1.html.

Note that for a paginated online article the full citation gives the URL for the first page. For rules regarding line breaks in URLs, see *10.8: Online publications*.

Opinions differ regarding inclusion of access dates. Since URLs and Internet sources may change over time, some authorities recommend including the last date that you verified the information by visiting the site. Others contend that such dates do not constitute proof of anything, and that they may mislead readers by appearing to indicate the date that the site was posted or updated. If you include access dates, clarify their meaning.

> Bain, Jennifer. "Hildegarde on 34th Street: Chant in the marketplace", *Echo* 6/1 (2004), http://www.echo.ucla.edu/volume6-issue1/bain/bain1.html (accessed 8 May 2006).

Other kinds of online publications are listed by author or editor whenever possible; otherwise they may be listed by organization. If a URL is very long, it may be shortened to that of the home page.

> [1] American Folklife Center, "About the American Folklife Center", http://www.loc.gov/folklife/aboutafc.html.

> [1] American Folklife Center, "About the American Folklife Center".

> [2] Harold S. Powers, et al., "Mode", *Grove music online*, ed. by Laura Macy, http://www.grovemusic.com.

> [2] Powers, et al., "Mode".

³ Ángel Romero, ed., "Malian guitar legend Ali Farka Toure dies at 67", *World music central,* http://www.worldmusiccentral.org.

³ Romero, ed., "Malian guitar legend Ali Farka Toure dies at 67".

These items are listed in the bibliography thus:

American Folklife Center. "About the American Folklife Center", http://www.loc.gov/folklife/aboutafc.html.

Powers, Harold S., et al., "Mode", *Grove music online*, ed. by Laura Macy, http://www.grovemusic.com.

Romero, Ángel, ed., "Malian guitar legend Ali Farka Toure dies at 67", *World music central,* http://www.worldmusiccentral.org.

Messages to listservs and other semipublic groups are cited like items in a collection, with the subject line as the item title, the group name as the collection title, and the sponsoring organization as the publisher:

¹ Alvaro Neder, "Re: Signification and meaning in music", *Society for Ethnomusicology discussion list*, 8 March 2006 (Bloomington: Society for Ethnomusicology).

¹ Neder, "Re: Signification and meaning in music".

This item is entered in the bibliography thus:

Neder, Alvaro. "Re: Signification and meaning in music", *Society for Ethnomusicology discussion list*, 8 March 2006 (Bloomington: Society for Ethnomusicology).

RILM abstracts are cited by their record numbers, which comprise two elements, separated by a hyphen: the year of the volume in which the record was published, and the five-digit number of that record in that volume.

1997-03797

The abstracts may be signed or unsigned. If an abstract is signed or credited to the author of the abstracted item, list it under that person's name. If the abstract is not by the author, include the author's name before the title of the abstracted item.

¹ Warren Kirkendale, abstract for his "Gregorianischer Stil in Beethovens Streichquartett op. 132", *RILM abstracts of music literature*, 1980-00564.

¹ Kirkendale, abstract for his "Gregorianischer Stil in Beethovens Streichquartett op. 132".

[2] Carl A. Skoggard, abstract for Burlasová *Vojenské a regrútské piesne, RILM abstracts of music literature,* 1993-06959.

[2] Skoggard, abstract for Burlasová *Vojenské a regrútské piesne.*

If the abstract is unsigned or credited to the publisher or journal, list it under *RILM abstracts of music literature*:

[3] *RILM abstracts of music literature,* abstract for Ferguson "Fis oder Fisis?", 1992-03797.

[3] *RILM*, abstract for Ferguson "Fis oder Fisis?"

These items are entered in the bibliography thus:

Kirkendale, Warren. Abstract for his "Gregorianischer Stil in Beethovens Streichquartett op. 132", *RILM abstracts of music literature,* 1980-00564.

Skoggard, Carl A. Abstract for Burlasová *Vojenské a regrútské piesne, RILM abstracts of music literature,* 1993-06959.

RILM abstracts of music literature. Abstract for Ferguson "Fis oder Fisis?", 1992-03797.

16.4.4 Correspondence

Published correspondence is cited like an item in a collection:

[1] Giuseppe Verdi, letter to Giulio Ricordi, 21 October 1883, *Carteggio Verdi–Ricordi, 1882–1885*, ed. by Franca Cella, Madina Ricordi, and Marisa Di Gregorio Casati (Parma: Istituto Nazionale di Studi Verdiani, 1994) 152–53.

[1] Verdi, letter to Giulio Ricordi, 21 October 1883.

This item is entered in the bibliography thus:

Verdi, Giuseppe. Letter to Giulio Ricordi, 21 October 1883, *Carteggio Verdi–Ricordi, 1882–1885*, ed. by Franca Cella, Madina Ricordi, and Marisa Di Gregorio Casati (Parma: Istituto Nazionale di Studi Verdiani, 1994) 152–53.

If you are citing several letters from the same book, you may choose to cite the book only once. When you cite the book as a whole, it should be listed by editor(s), not by the author(s) of the letters:

[1] Cella, et al., 152–53.

In this case, the book is entered in the bibliography thus:

Cella, Franca, Madina Ricordi, and Marisa Di Gregorio Casati, eds. *Carteggio Verdi–Ricordi, 1882–1885* (Parma: Istituto Nazionale di Studi Verdiani, 1994).

Correspondence published online is cited with the appropriate URL:

[2] Fred McCormick, "Re: Eddie Butcher review", *Musical traditions*, 13 February 2006, http://www.mustrad.org.uk/letters.htm.

[2] McCormick, "Re: Eddie Butcher review".

This item is entered in the bibliography thus:

McCormick, Fred, "Re: Eddie Butcher review", *Musical traditions*, 13 February 2006, http://www.mustrad.org.uk/letters.htm.

For messages to listservs and other semipublic groups, see *16.4.3.2: Online publications*.

Unpublished correspondence is cited with information on where the correspondence is kept:

[1] Félix Alexandre Guilmant, letter to Emil Sjögren, 20 June 1908. Stockholm: Nordiska Museet, Emil Sjögrens Arkiv, MS 129.1945.

[1] Guilmant, letter to Emil Sjögren, 20 June 1908.

This item is entered in the bibliography thus:

Guilmant, Félix Alexandre. Letter to Emil Sjögren, 20 June 1908. Stockholm: Nordiska Museet, Emil Sjögrens Arkiv, MS 129. 1945.

Private e-mails may be cited without titles or location information:

[2] Dorothea Hast, e-mail to the author, 17 March 2006.

[2] Hast, e-mail to the author, 17 March 2006.

This item is entered in the bibliography thus:

Hast, Dorothea. E-mail to the author, 17 March 2006.

16.4.5 Manuscripts and collections

Manuscripts may be referred to in the text without notes, or they may be cited in notes thus:

[1] Berlin, Staatsbibliothek, Cod.gr.174.

They are listed in a separate bibliography or index according to where they are kept, by city, institution, and shelf number (former shelf numbers are indicated in parentheses with the word *olim*). Additional information—author, true title, generic title, date, and so on—may follow the shelf number in brackets:

Berlin, Staatsbibliothek
 Cod.gr.174 [Phillipps 1577]

Bruxelles, Bibliothèque Royale Albert Ier
 9392 [Christine de Pizan, *L'Epître d'Othéa*]
 10607 [Psalter of Guy de Dampierre, Count of Flanders]

Milano, Archivio Storico Ricordi (Casa Editrice)
 M.1.13 [Donizetti *Don Pasquale* autograph]

Trento, Museo Nazionale (Castello del Buonconsiglio)
 1374–79 (*olim* 87–92) [Trent Codices]

New York, The Pierpont Morgan Library
 G.25
 M.788 [*Matāli ʿal-Saʿāda*]

Other items in collections are handled similarly:

[2] Vermillion, National Music Museum, NMM.4457.

Vermillion, National Music Museum
 NMM.4457 [hardingfele, Norway, 18th/19th century]
 NMM.7129 [William Lander, serpent in C]

[3] Washington, D.C., Archive of Folk Culture, AFS 4423–4427.

Washington, D.C., Archive of Folk Culture
 AFS 4423–4427 [Alan Lomax, field recordings of Philias Bedard, 1941]
 AFS 13,577–13,671 [Robert W. Gordon, field recordings ca. 1929–1932]

Unpublished recordings in personal collections are listed by composer, performer, or place, as appropriate:

[4] Tyāgarāja, *Kaligiyuṇṭē*. Tanjore Brinda, voice; Tanjore Viswanathan, flute; Tanjore Ranganathan, mṛdaṅgam. Tape recording by Matthew Harp Allen, Madras, 1977.

[4] Tyāgarāja, *Kaligiyuṇṭē*.

[5] García Villamil, Felipe, interview by the author. Video tape recording, Bronx, 1998.

[5] García Villamil, interview.

[6] Central African Republic, *Makala*, Aka people. Tape recording by Michelle Kisliuk, 1988.

[6] Central African Republic, *Makala*.

These may be listed along with published sound recordings or in a separate section.

Tyāgarāja. *Kaligiyuṇṭē*. Tanjore Brinda, voice; Tanjore Viswanathan, flute; Tanjore Ranganathan, mṛdaṅgam. Tape recording by Matthew Harp Allen, Madras. 1977.

García Villamil, Felipe, interview by the author. Video tape recording, Bronx, 1998.

Central African Republic. *Makala*. Aka people. Tape recording by Michelle Kisliuk, 1988.

16.5 In-text citations and bibliographic formats

These are parenthetical references inserted into the text instead of numbered notes. They are always linked to a bibliography; full citations are never given in parentheses. Only the author's last name, the date of publication, and the pagination is given. These should immediately follow run-in quotations. For block quotations, they follow end punctuation. For prose references or paraphrases, they are best placed at the end of sentences, before end punctuation; if this would cause confusion, they may be placed in the body of the sentence. These examples represent the same sources as the ones in section *16.4: Numbered notes and bibliographic formats.*

16.5.1 Printed materials

The in-text citation form is the same for monographs, articles, essays, theses, and dissertations:

> (Nettl 2002:125)
>
> (Best 2004:23)
>
> (Farkas 1997:61)

Ibid. may be used for the work cited in the immediately preceding note:

> (Ibid., 126–27)

The cumbersome and potentially misleading *op. cit.* and *loc. cit.* are eschewed.

In-text citations are inserted at the appropriate point in the text; often this will be at the end of a quotation or paraphrase. If the author's name appears in the text it is omitted from the citation, which will usually follow the author's name to avoid confusion:

> Hess (2001:63) notes the influence of Falla's obituary for Granados.

The above items are entered in the bibliography thus:

> Nettl, Bruno. 2002. *Encounters in ethnomusicology: A memoir* (Warren, Mich.: Harmonie Park Press).
>
> Best, David. 2004. "Relationships: Musical and personal—Theme and variations", *International journal of music education* 22/1:21–33.

Farkas, Ferenc. 1997. "Kodály és a magyar műdal", *Kodály emlékkönyv 1997*, ed. by Ferenc Bónis. Magyar zenetörténeti tanulmányok 7 (Budapest: Püski) 60–63.

Hess, Carol A. 2001. *Manuel de Falla and modernism in Spain, 1898–1936* (University of Chicago Press).

Note that end punctuation goes outside quotation marks: End punctuation goes inside quotation marks only when it is part of the title (see *2.11.3: End punctuation with quotation marks*). Titles that include end punctuation are not followed by a period or comma:

Neumann, Alfred E. 1997. "What, me wordy?" *Pomo review* 21/108: 23–55.

Note also that in the Farkas example the series information is given before the publisher.

In some situations you may wish to give additional information:

Lassiter, Luke E. 1998. *The power of Kiowa song: A collaborative ethnography* (Tucson: University of Arizona Press) xv, 266 p. ISBN 0-8165-1835-1. Illus., port., bibliog., index, tables, diagr., maps.

When multiple works by an author are listed, the author's name is replaced by five underscores after the first listing:

Nettl, Bruno. 1995. *Heartland excursions: Ethnomusicological reflections on schools of music* (Urbana: University of Illinois Press).

_____. 2002. *Encounters in ethnomusicology: A memoir* (Warren, Mich.: Harmonie Park Press).

Note that works by the same author are arranged chronologically, not alphabetically by title.

Multiple items by the same author from the same year are alphabetized by title, and sequential letters are added to the dates:

Nettl, Bruno. 2002a. "Alexander L. Ringer (1921–2002)". *SEM newsletter* 36/4:21.

_____. 2002b. *Encounters in ethnomusicology: A memoir* (Warren, Mich.: Harmonie Park Press).

The in-text citation reflects this addition:

(Nettl 2002b:125)

Translations and editions other than the first are indicated thus:

> Touma, Habib Hassan. 1996. *The music of the Arabs*. Trans. by
> Laurie Schwartz (Rev. ed.; Portland, Ore.: Amadeus).

Some books are issued simultaneously by two publishers:

> Reichling, Alfred, ed. 2001. *Orgel*. MGG prisma; Veröffentlichung
> der Gesellschaft der Orgelfreunde 181 (Kassel: Bärenreiter;
> Stuttgart: Metzler).

Note that the series information (two series, in this case) is given after the title.

The practice of treating dissertations and theses as writings that do not merit the same treatment as published ones is gratuitously demeaning. Especially now that anyone with a computer and a printer can be a print publisher and anyone with Internet access can be an online publisher, the fact that a piece of writing has been published should not confer more status than the fact that an extended study has been accepted by a committee of recognized experts on its subject. Dissertations and theses exist in the same form as print publications—as books—and copies may be found at the granting institutions and, not infrequently, at other libraries. Titles should be italicized, and the designation *unpublished* should be omitted. Degree-granting institutions are treated similarly to publishers.

> Griffiths, Mikaela Ceridwen. 2003. *A profile of needs: Music ther-*
> *apy with HIV infected children in a South African institution*
> (M.Mus. thesis, University of Pretoria).

16.5.1.1 Reference publications and tertiary sources

Entries in reference publications and tertiary sources are seldom cited; however, in some cases they are the only available sources—for example, when nothing else has been published on a topic, or when a publication cannot be located or is in an unfamiliar language. In rare cases, a tertiary source may provide the most current or comprehensive published treatment of a topic. For online versions of such sources, see *16.5.3: Electronic publications*.

These are treated like items in a collection. If they are signed, they are entered under the author's name; if they are unsigned, they are entered under the editor's name.

(Miranda-Pérez 2002)

(Powers, et al. 2001:842)

(Larkin, ed. 1995:4578)

These items are entered in the bibliography thus:

Miranda-Pérez, Ricardo. 2002. "Herrera de la Puente, Luis", *Die Musik in Geschichte und Gegenwart: Personenteil*, ed. by Ludwig Finscher (2nd ed. rev.; Kassel: Bärenreiter; Stuttgart: Metzler) vol. 8, 1421.

Powers, Harold S., et al. 2001. "Mode", *The new Grove dictionary of music and musicians*, ed. by Stanley Sadie (2nd ed. rev.; London: Macmillan; New York: Grove's Dictionaries) vol. 16, 775–860.

Larkin, Colin, ed. 1995. "Yamaguchi, Momoe", *The Guinness encyclopedia of popular music* (2nd ed.; Middlesex: Guinness; New York: Stockton) vol. 6, 4578.

Note that edition information is given in parentheses with the publisher information.

RILM abstracts in print are cited the same way as those in online sources; see *16.5.3: Electronic publications*.

16.5.1.2 Notes and commentary in scores and editions

These are treated like items in collections:

(Strauss 1942:3)

(Jacobs 1983:152)

These items are entered in the bibliography thus:

Strauss, Richard. 1942. "Geleitwort", *Capriccio* by Clemens Kraus and Richard Strauss (Mainz: B. Schotts; London: Boosey & Hawkes) 1–4.

Jacobs, Charles. 1983. "Critical notes", *Frescobaldi's "Il primo libro de madrigali a cinque voci"*, ed. by Charles Jacobs (University Park; London: Pennsylvania State University Press) 151–57.

Note that if you are citing the second example as an edition (as opposed to only citing the editor's notes) it is listed under the composer's name, not the editor's; see *16.5.1.6: Editions of music.*

16.5.1.3 Reviews

These are treated as articles. Untitled reviews are listed with a brief description instead of a title.

> Ross, Alex. 2001. "Resurrection: The Passion according to Osvaldo Golijov", *The New Yorker* 77/2 (5 March):100–01.

> Avorgbedor, Daniel. 2005. Review of Charry *Mande music*, in *The world of music* 47/2:163–67.

Note that for the second example the word *in* is added for clarity.

16.5.1.4 Liner notes

Some liner notes have titles other than the title of the recording; many do not. In either case, citations should state that they are liner notes and give basic publishing data for the recording:

> Frühauf, Tina. 2002. "Introduction to the libretto/Introduction du livret/Vorwort zum Libretto". Liner notes for *Charles Gounod: Faust* (Andante 3995) 54 57; 116–19; 182–86.

> Hentoff, Nat. 1963. Liner notes for *The freewheelin' Bob Dylan* (Columbia Records CS 8786).

Sometimes supplements, updates, or errata for liner notes may be found online; these are treated as online publications (see *16.5.3: Electronic publications*). Full publishing data for the original publication is not necessary, but the owner or sponsor of the website should be noted. The year of the online publication is given, not that of the original recording.

> Yamplosky, Philip. 1998. "Liner notes supplements: What is a gamelan?". http://www.folkways.si.edu/projects_initiatives/indonesian/liner_notes/volume14.html (Smithsonian Folkways Recordings).

For rules regarding line breaks in URLs, see *10.8: Online publications.*

16.5.1.5 Program notes

These are issued in various forms. Some, like *Stagebill*, are issued as periodicals; these are treated as such in bibliographies, and the program notes are treated like articles. Others are issued as books, with changeable details—such as lists of performers—provided as an insert; these are treated like collections of essays. For these two cases, see *16.5.1: Printed materials*.

For notes in programs that are neither periodicals nor collections, titles of notes and programs are given when they appear, as is the performance date or date range. The sponsoring organization or venue may serve as the publisher. The publication may or may not be paginated.

> Rostand, Claude. 1972. "Jean Rivier: 7ᵉ symphonie en fa". Program notes for Orchestre de Paris, 22–25 March (Paris: Société des Concerts du Conservatoire).

> Block, Adrienne Fried. 2002. "The Philharmonic promotes chamber music, 1843–68". Program notes for *The New York Philharmonic ensembles in a historically informed program of chamber music*, 2 December (New York: City University of New York) 1–4.

> Rosenthal, Harold. 1971. Program notes for *Tristan und Isolde* by Richard Wagner, 3 July (London: Royal Opera House Covent Garden).

16.5.1.6 Editions of music

Works are not cited bibliographically or in notes unless a particular edition is discussed:

(Vittori 2002)

The item is entered in the bibliography thus:

> Vittori, Loreto. 2002. *La Galatea*. Ed. by Thomas D. Dunn (Middleton, Wis.: A-R Editions).

Note that the composer is the author; the editor's name follows the title.

For multivolume editions of complete works, series information is given after the title. The item is entered in the bibliography thus:

> Händel, Georg Friedrich. 1999. *Israel in Egypt, HWV 54*. Hallische Händel-Ausgabe: Kritische Gesamtausgabe I—Oratorien und große Kantaten 14 (Kassel: Bärenreiter; Stuttgart: Metzler).

Exceptionally, critical editions published as part of a dissertation or thesis are listed under the name of the editor/author.

> Spence, Marcia Louise. 1995. *Carl Nielsen's quintet for winds, op. 43: A critical edition* (DMA diss., University of North Texas).

For items in the volume other than the work itself, see *16.5.1.2: Notes and commentary in scores and editions*.

16.5.1.7 Technical drawings of instruments

The person who made the drawing is treated as the author:

> (Vromans 1988)

In the bibliography, titles are in standardized form, in English, giving the instrument type and maker (*Anonymous* when necessary), with the place and date (approximate, if necessary) in parentheses. The location of the instrument is indicated, including the inventory number in the collection. The date of the drawing is given, even if it is the same as the publication date, and the number of sheets is noted.

> Vromans, Fer. 1988. *Barrel organ by Diederik Nicolaus Winkel* (Amsterdam, ca. 1820). Owned by Haags Gemeentemuseum, Ea 178-X-1952. Drawn in 1988. 6 sheets ('s-Gravenhage: Haags Gemeentemuseum.

16.5.2 Audio and audiovisual materials

Mass-media publishers are often not associated with a single city, and the location of their executive offices may not be relevant. In such cases, do not force a place name.

16.5.2.1 Sound recordings

Recordings may be listed in a discography; they should be cited only if they are discussed in the text. References may be given by composer, performer, producer, or compiler as appropriate:

> (Bartók 1979)
>
> (Parton 2001)
>
> (Broadbank and Bor 1999)
>
> (Lomax 1999)

These are entered in the discography thus:

Bartók, Béla. 1979. *Pour les enfants.* Michel Béroff, piano. 2 LPs;
includes other Bartók piano works (EMI La Voix de Son Maître 2C
167-16.246/247).

Parton, Dolly. 2001. *Little sparrow.* CD (Sugar Hill Records 3927).

Broadbank, Robin, and Joep Bor, prods. 1999. *The raga guide: A
survey of 74 Hindustani ragas.* 4 CDs (Nimbus 5536–5539).

Lomax, Alan, comp. 1999. *Carriacou Calaloo.* The Alan Lomax
collection: Caribbean voyage. CD (Rounder Records 1722).

Note that for the Bartók example the work title is given as it appears on
the sound recording itself; it is not changed to its original language.

There is no need to cite individual tracks in notes; specific sections, titles,
etc., are supplied in the text:

Parton has even recorded standards such as Cole Porter's "I get a
kick out of you" (Parton 2001).

For liner notes, see *16.5.1.4: Liner notes.*

16.5.2.2 Films and video recordings

Films and video recordings may be listed in a filmography or
videography (the two may be combined); they should be cited only if
they are discussed in the text. They are treated like books, with an indication of the medium for the full citation. References may be given by composer, director, producer(s), or title as appropriate:

(Verdi 2003)

(Hitchcock 1998)

(Evans, Ferris, and Peiser 1971)

(*Noreg i dans og spel* 2002)

Feature films are treated similarly to musical works: They are only cited
when a specific edition is under discussion. So, for example, *Psycho*
need not be cited as a publication if the reference is to Bernard Herrmann's score for the film; however, if the reference is to one of the additional features added for the DVD edition, the above citation is in order.

These are entered in the filmography or videography thus:

> Verdi, Giuseppe. 2003. *Nabucco*. DVD. Teatro alla Scala, Riccardo Muti, conductor (Kultur D2042).

> Hitchcock, Alfred. 1998. *Psycho*. DVD (MCA Home Video).

> Evans, David, William Ferris, and Judy Peiser. 1971. *Gravel Springs fife and drum*. 16mm (Memphis: Center for Southern Folklore).

> *Noreg i dans og spel*. 2002. VHS (Dragvoll: Rådet for Folkemusikk og Folkedans).

16.5.2.3 Music videos

These are generally treated like films and videos, listed by performer:

> (Quintanilla Pérez 1992)

> (Outkast 2003)

These items are entered in the videography thus:

> Quintanilla Pérez, Selena. 1992. *La carcacha*. VHS (EMI Latin).

> Outkast. 2003. *Hey ya*. DVD (La Face).

Note that Selena is listed under her full name, not her stage name. When necessary, the stage name follows the full name in parentheses. See *9.1.3: Name changes, pseudonyms, and sobriquets*.

16.5.2.4 Radio and television broadcasts

Typography for titles should be slightly different than it is in prose: Treat both ongoing programs and single ones as works, and treat series as institutions (see *8.1: When to capitalize*). Like films, they may be grouped by composer, director, producer(s), or title as appropriate:

> (Stockhausen 2005)

> (Monsaingeon 2005)

> (*The Ed Sullivan show* 1964)

These items are entered in the bibliography thus:

> Stockhausen, Karlheinz. 2005. *Mittwochs-Gruß* (BBC Radio 3, 27 August).

Monsaingeon, Bruno. 2005. *The art of the violin* (Great Performances, PBS, 22 May).

The Ed Sullivan show. 1964. (CBS, 9 February).

16.5.3 Electronic publications

These are treated just like printed writings:

(Rich 1992)

(Bain 2004:3)

(Powers, et al. n.d.)

(Romero, ed. n.d.)

Articles in online journals are not always paginated; the second example above points to an article that appears on a sequence of five Web pages. If a URL is very long it may be shortened to that of the home page.

Items from websites that are continually updated are cited as *n.d.* (no date). An access date may be included (see below), but it should not be treated as the publication date.

Where no author or editor is indicated, an organization may be used:

(American Folklife Center n.d.)

These are entered in the bibliography thus:

Rich, Alan. 1992. *Bach and before: A collector's guide to compact discs*. CD-ROM (Santa Monica: Voyager).

Bain, Jennifer. 2004. "Hildegarde on 34th Street: Chant in the marketplace", *Echo* 6/1, http://www.echo.ucla.edu/volume6-issue1/bain/bain3.html.

American Folklife Center. n.d. "About the American Folklife Center", http://www.loc.gov/folklife/aboutafc.html.

Powers, Harold S., et al. n.d. "Mode", *Grove music online*, ed. by Laura Macy, http://www.grovemusic.com.

Romero, Ángel, ed. n.d. "Malian guitar legend Ali Farka Toure dies at 67", *World music central,* http://www.worldmusiccentral.org.

Opinions differ regarding inclusion of access dates. Since URLs and Internet sources may change over time, some authorities recommend including the last date that you verified the information by visiting the site.

Others contend that such dates do not constitute proof of anything, and that they may mislead readers by appearing to indicate the date that the site was posted or updated. If you include access dates, clarify their meaning.

> Bain, Jennifer. 2004. "Hildegarde on 34th Street: Chant in the marketplace", *Echo* 6/1, http://www.echo.ucla.edu/volume6-issue1/bain/bain1.html (accessed 8 May 2006).

For rules regarding line breaks in URLs, see *10.8: Online publications.*

Messages to listservs and other semipublic groups are cited like items in a collection, with the subject line as the item title, the group name as the collection title, and the sponsoring organization as the publisher:

> (Neder 2006)

> Neder, Alvaro. 2006. "Re: Signification and meaning in music", *Society for Ethnomusicology discussion list* (Bloomington: Society for Ethnomusicology).

RILM abstracts are cited by their record numbers, which contain two elements, separated by a hyphen: the year of the volume in which the record was published, and the five-digit number of that record in that volume.

> 1997-03197

The abstracts may be signed or unsigned. If an abstract is signed or credited to the author of the abstracted item, list it under that person's name.

> (Kirkendale 1980)

> (Skoggard 1993)

If the abstract is unsigned or credited to the publisher or journal, give the record number:

> (RILM 1992-03797)

These items are entered in the bibliography thus:

> Kirkendale, Warren. 1980. Abstract for his "Gregorianischer Stil in Beethovens Streichquartett op. 132", *RILM abstracts of music literature*, 1980-00564.

> Skoggard, Carl A. 1993. Abstract for Burlasová *Vojenské a regrútské piesne*, *RILM abstracts of music literature*, 1993-06959.

> *RILM abstracts of music literature*. 1992. Abstract for Ferguson "Fis oder Fisis?", 1992-03797.

16.5.4 Correspondence

Published correspondence is cited like an item in a collection:

(Verdi 1883)

Note that Verdi's letter is cited with the date of the letter itself. Since several letters—including unpublished ones—may be cited in the same item, it is best to cite all correspondence this way.

This item is entered in the bibliography thus:

> Verdi, Giuseppe. 1883. Letter to Giulio Ricordi, 21 October, *Carteggio Verdi–Ricordi, 1882–1885*, ed. by Franca Cella, Madina Ricordi, and Marisa Di Gregorio Casati (Parma: Istituto Nazionale di Studi Verdiani, 1994) 152–53.

If you are citing several letters from the same book, you may choose to cite the book only once. When you cite the book as a whole, it should be listed by editor(s), not by the author(s) of the letters:

(Cella, et al. 1994:152–53)

In this case, the book is entered in the bibliography thus:

> Cella, Franca, Madina Ricordi, and Marisa Di Gregorio Casati, eds. 1994. *Carteggio Verdi–Ricordi, 1882–1885* (Parma: Istituto Nazionale di Studi Verdiani).

Correspondence published online is cited with the appropriate URL:

(McCormick 2006)

> McCormick, Fred. 2006. "Re: Eddie Butcher review", *Musical traditions*, 13 February, http://www.mustrad.org.uk/letters.htm.

For messages to listservs and other semipublic groups, see *16.5.3: Electronic publications*.

Unpublished correspondence is cited with information on where the correspondence is kept:

(Guilmant 1908)

> Guilmant, Félix Alexandre. 1908. Letter to Emil Sjögren, 20 June. Stockholm: Nordiska Museet, Emil Sjögrens Arkiv, MS 129.1945.

Private e-mails may be cited without titles or location information:

(Hast 2006)

Hast, Dorothea. 2006. E-mail to the author, 17 March.

16.5.5 Manuscripts and collections

Manuscripts may be referred to in the text without parenthetical citations, or they may be cited thus:

(Berlin, Staatsbibliothek, Cod.gr.174)

They are listed in a separate bibliography or index according to where they are kept, by city, institution, and shelf number (former shelf numbers are indicated in parentheses with the word *olim*). Additional information—author, true title, generic title, date, and so on—may follow the shelf number in brackets:

Berlin, Staatsbibliothek, Preußischer Kulturbesitz
    Cod.gr.174 [Phillipps 1577]

Bruxelles, Bibliothèque Royale Albert Ier
    9392 [Christine de Pizan, *L'Epître d'Othéa*]
    10607 [Psalter of Guy de Dampierre, Count of Flanders]

Milano, Archivio Storico Ricordi (Casa Editrice)
    M.1.13 [Donizetti *Don Pasquale* autograph]

Trento, Museo Nazionale (Castello del Buonconsiglio)
    1374–79 (*olim* 87–92) [Trent Codices]

New York, The Pierpont Morgan Library
    G.25
    M.788 [*Matāli 'al-Sa'āda*]

Other items in collections are handled similarly:

(Vermillion, National Music Museum, NMM.4457)

Vermillion, National Music Museum
    NMM.4457 [hardingfele, Norway, 18th/19th century]
    NMM.7129 [William Lander, serpent in C]

(Washington, D.C., Archive of Folk Culture, AFS 4423–4427)

Washington, D.C., Archive of Folk Culture

    AFS 4423–4427 [Alan Lomax, field recordings of Philias
      Bedard, 1941]
    AFS 13,577–13,671 [Robert W. Gordon, field recordings ca.
      1929–1932]

Unpublished recordings in personal collections are listed by composer, performer, or place, as appropriate:

(Tyāgarāja 1977)

(García Villamil 1998)

(Central African Republic 1988)

These may be listed along with published recordings or in a separate section.

Tyāgarāja. 1977. *Kaligiyuṇṭē*. Tanjore Brinda, voice; Tanjore Viswanathan, flute; Tanjore Ranganathan, mṛdaṅgam. Tape recording by Matthew Harp Allen, Madras.

García Villamil, Felipe. 1998. Interview by the author. Video tape recording, Bronx.

Central African Republic. 1988. *Makala*. Aka people. Tape recording by Michelle Kisliuk.

17. INDEXING

Indexes provide crucial access to information; they are indispensable features of most nonfiction books. But vague indexes that force readers to flip back and forth, laboriously searching for the nuggets of information they need, are all too common. Few scholarly publishers provide professional indexing for monographs; authors are usually told that if they want an index they will have to supply it themselves. Understandably, indexes prepared by amateurs are seldom ideal.

RILM's indexing system, developed to help users sift through hundreds of thousands of entries, is much too complex for indexing a single book; still, many of the insights we have arrived at will be useful for the novice indexer. Below you will find some basic information on how RILM approaches indexing, and some models that you may choose to follow. Depending on what your book covers, you may want to provide separate indexes for personal names, topics, titles, manuscripts, and so on. (For indexing manuscripts and items in collections, see *16.4.5* or *16.5.5: Manuscripts and collections*.)

17.1 Getting started

Before the advent of word processing, one way to begin indexing was to divide several sheets of paper into sections, one for each letter of the alphabet. As indexers read through final page proofs, they wrote topics and page numbers in the appropriate letter sections, adding new page numbers to topics whenever they reappeared in the text; the next phase was alphabetizing topics under each letter. Larger or more detailed indexes were compiled using index cards. If you do not have access to a computer, you may compile your index in one of these time-honored ways.

If you have access to a computer, it may already have indexing software that will alphabetize listings and perform other organizational chores. If not, open a new document and type each letter of the alphabet on a new line, with three blank lines under it. As you go through your final page proof, enter each new topic and page number on a blank line under the appropriate letter, adding a new blank line for the next one; alphabetize as you go along. Add new page numbers to topics when they come up again. After one pass through your page proof you will have a rudimentary index.

17.2 Headwords

In indexing parlance, the topics you have compiled are *headwords*. Typically these are terms, phrases, or names that someone might want to look up in your book. You might be surprised by what some people will look for, so try to select as wide a range of headwords as possible. In addition to topics, it is best to index every person and organization mentioned in your text, and it will probably be worthwhile to index most place names.

17.2.1 See references

If readers are likely to look for something under a headword that you have chosen not to use, a *see reference* can send them to the right place. For example, if you index the rock musician Bono under his full name, you can include a see reference that will alphabetize under *B*; see references may also be useful for places and topics.

Bono *see* **Hewson, Paul (Bono)**

South Asia *see* **Asia, South**

bebop *see* **jazz**

17.3 Second levels

If a personal name, for example, only occurs once or twice in your book, there is no need to add more detail to it in the index; anyone who has looked for that name will probably want to read the passages where it appears. If, however, several references to that name are indicated by several page numbers following it in the index, readers will be grateful if you provide more information by adding second levels that are indented and alphabetized under the headword.

For example, someone who is only interested in Cherubini's operas will thank you for this level of specificity:

Cherubini, Luigi
    cantatas
    hymns
    Masses
    operas
    overtures
    string quartets

Similarly, someone looking for information on Chilean instruments will appreciate this breakdown:

Chile
   history
   instruments
   pedagogy
   politics
   popular music
   traditional music

Of course, these are hypothetical categories. Always think in terms of balancing the most accurate characterization with the needs of people who may consult your index. If Cherubini is a minor figure in your book and general aspects of his works are touched upon in various places in it, the above indexing may suffice. If, however, your book is about the life and works of Cherubini, more detailed indexing is called for; when this is the case, you will want to establish margin terms.

17.4 Margin terms and subsequent levels

Margin terms are fixed subheadings, usually placed on second levels so they line up in the margin under the headword (exceptions are noted under *17.4.2: Places*). Further levels are grouped and indented under these margin terms, so the index is clearly organized and easy to read. RILM margin terms and their uses are outlined below; you are welcome to adopt any or all of them, or you may find that it makes sense to devise ones that are more appropriate for your book.

17.4.1 Personal names

Example 1 presents RILM's margin terms for personal names in three groups: *most specific*, *more general*, and *most general*. If a concept can be appropriately grouped under more than one of these terms, it is best to choose the least general one; the more general margin terms tend to group more subheadings, making individual entries harder to locate. So, for example, a passage referring to manuscripts of a composer's works could be indexed under *works*, but *manuscripts* is preferred because it is more specific. Similarly, since a Festschrift is a type of tribute, it could be indexed under *tributes*, but *Festschriften* is more specific.

Ex. 1: Personal Margin Terms

Most specific	**More general**	**Most general**
bibliographies	collections	aesthetics
catalogues	correspondence	life
chronologies	editions	works
discographies	iconography	writings
exhibitions	instruments	
festivals and conferences	manuscripts	
Festschriften	performances	
filmographies	reception	
interviews	sound recordings	
obituaries	tributes	
periodicals		
transcriptions		
translations		
videographies		

Our use of standarized phrases in indexing is also hierarchical (see examples 2 and 3). For example, the phrase openings *compared with, influence on,* and *influenced by* denote more specific connections than *relation to*; the latter is used for more complex interrelationships. Standardizing the openings of such phrases clarifies the index, since phrases with the same openings will be alphabetized together.

Example 2 presents some RILM indexing for a popular musician; example 3 presents indexing for a composer. Note that in example 3 the margin term *performances* is used both for performances by Bartók and for performances of his works by others. Note also that the titles of his works and writings are given in the original language. Since readers of a book written in English may not recognize the Hungarian titles, they are followed by parenthetical translations (see *10.1.2: Translations*).

For information on the treatment of personal names, including alphabetization, stage names, and other considerations, see *9.1: Names of people.*

Ex. 2: Indexing for Madonna

Ciccone, Madonna Louise
bibliographies
discographies
    to 2005
iconography
    magazine covers
interviews
life
    career
    persona
        relation to feminism
        relation to mass media
    relation to Spears
    views on religion
performances
    Blonde ambition tour
        costumes
    Evita
    gestural analysis
    influence on Trevi
    influenced by hard rock
    music videos
        Justify my love
        Material girl
    role of parody and pastiche
reception
    academic vs. journalistic writings
    France
    relation to visual images
    women
sound recordings
    compared with music videos
    influenced by techno
    Ray of light
videographies
works
    feminist interpretations
    Papa, don't preach
    1980s
writings
    song lyrics

Ex. 3: Indexing for Bartók

Bartók, Béla
aesthetics
    influenced by traditional music
    modernism
correspondence
    from Doflein
    to Verhuyck
festivals and conferences
    Hungary
        Miskolc, 2005
        Szombathely, 2000
life
    last years
    relation to Kodály
    teaching of Csikor
performance practice
    Contrasts
    piano music
performances
    A csodálatos mandarin (The miraculous mandarin)
        by Harangozó
        premiere, 1927
    European tour, 1922
    Schubert works
reception
    Hungary
    1945 to present
transcriptions
    Transylvanian traditional music
    use of special signs
writings
    A magyar népzene (Hungarian traditional music)
    Hungarian song classification
    on Strauss
works
    choral music
    Gyermekeknek (For children)
    influence on Ligeti
    influenced by Grieg
    viewed by Hindemith

17.4.2 Places

Example 4 presents RILM's geographic margin terms, which are grouped and prioritized the same way that our personal margin terms are. However, there is one difference in the way these are handled: Geographic information may be given in more than one level, pushing the margin term to whatever level follows the geographic levels. So, for example, if your book is about musical life in North America in the 19th century, your index might include this very general entry, in which the margin term *musical life* appears in the second level:

North America
    musical life
        community organizations

It also might include a much more specific entry, such as this:

Canada
    Ontario
    Toronto
        musical life
            reception of Wagner

In the second example, the same margin term is pushed to the fourth level, following the hierarchically ordered geographic information. Note that **Canada** is the headword, rather than **North America**; there is no need to situate Canada by continent in the index. However, for a book like this it is a good idea to group cities by country and province or state; the index will be more organized and easier to use. For a book with less information about Canada, the province may be omitted. Note also that there is no need to include the qualifier *19th century*, since that is the stated time frame covered by the book.

RILM also puts ethnic information before the margin term. While ethnic and geographic considerations are not analogous, we have learned that this practice proves useful.

    United States of America
        Arizona
            Tohono O'odham people
                dance
                    waila
                instruments
                traditional music
                    fiddle music

Ex. 4: Geographic margin terms

Most specific	More general	Most general
antiquity	blues	aesthetics
bibliographies	cultural policies	culture
catalogues	economics	dance
discographies	ethnomusicology	dramatic arts
filmographies	iconography	folklore
periodicals	instruments	history
videographies	jazz	history of music
	librarianship	literature
	mass media	musical life
	musicology	popular music
	pedagogy	traditional music
	performance practice	visual and plastic arts
	politics	
	religious music	
	sociology	
	theory	

Some of our geographic margin terms may need explanation. RILM uses *history of music* instead of *classical music* or *art music*, and we use *traditional music* instead of *folk music*. Both *history of music* and *traditional music* are applied to non-Western cultures as well as to Western ones. So, for example, Japanese koto repertoire is indexed under *history of music*, as are Japanese contemporary composers; Japanese folk songs are indexed under *traditional music*. We adopted the margin terms *blues* and *jazz* because opinions differ as to whether blues is popular or traditional music, and whether jazz is popular or art music. We use the margin terms *musicology* and *ethnomusicology* only for items about those disciplines, not for items about the musics studied by musicologists or ethnomusicologists.

Example 5 presents some margin-term indexing for a place. Note that Chinese-language titles and genre terms are used; where translations might be helpful, they are supplied in parentheses.

Ex. 5: Indexing for China

China
antiquity
    instruments
    ritual music
        viewed by Confucius
culture
    influence on Southeast Asia
    viewed by Jesuits
dramatic arts
    jingju (Beijing opera)
    yueju (Cantonese opera)
ethnomusicology
    conferences
    publications
        journals
history of music
    guqin music
    late 20th century
Huzhu
    Monguor people
        traditional music
            instrumental music
            wedding songs
instruments
    erhu
    wind
musical life
    festivals
    Tang dynasty
northwestern
    traditional music
        hua'er
        shaonian
politics
    Cultural Revolution
    influence on jingju
popular music
    rock
    ca. 2000
traditional music
    children's songs
    Ketu qiuhen (Autumn regret of the exile's road)
    sound recordings

Note that—following the rule about preferring the most specific margin term—*instruments* appears under the margin term *antiquity*, but *instruments* also appears as a margin term itself when a more specific category is not indicated.

17.4.3 Topics

Topic indexing is not as pre-defined as that for people and places, and to some extent it must be handled on a case-by-case basis. Use precise terms for topics that are covered extensively, allowing more general terms for topics that may be grouped together. For example, in a book about jazz saxophonists it may make sense to list players separately by their favored instrument—soprano, alto, tenor, baritone, or bass—while a more general book about jazz may not require such detailed indexing.

A list of topical headwords currently used by RILM may be viewed at http://www.rilm.org/headwords.html. This list comprises more headwords than any single book would require, but it provides examples of the kinds of topics you might consider.

For extensive indexing under a single topic, you may wish to establish appropriate margin terms. For example, listings under **pedagogy** could be sorted by level (*elementary, secondary*, etc.), by subtopic (*composition, piano playing*, etc.), by population (*amateurs, children*, etc.), by place, or by some combination of these.

Example 6 presents some RILM indexing for a topic, using five margin terms that we established as ways of organizing items about the two main disciplines we cover: musicology and ethnomusicology. Rules governing their use keep things in order. For example, place names can only appear under *academic activities* and *national and regional studies*; *as discipline* is only for topics, never for people or places; *research tools and techniques* is only for specific considerations, not for general items about methodology (these go under *as discipline*); and *publications* is only for general items about publications, not for individual publications themselves (the rare exceptions include discussions of ongoing work on critical editions or anthologies).

Ex. 6: Indexing for ethnomusicology

ethnomusicology
    academic activities
        conferences
        Germany
            Berlin
            partnership with Brazil, 1990
        Hungary
            activities of Kodály
    as discipline
        applied ethnomusicology
        compared with musicology
        concept of soundscape
        emic vs. etic perspective
        methodology
            relation to sociology
    national and regional studies
        Africa
            historiography
            sub-Saharan
        India
            women's studies
            19th century
        Pacific Rim
            state of research
    publications
        bibliography
        Croatia
        sound recordings
    research tools and techniques
        analysis
        computer applications
            rhythmic analysis
        fieldwork
        transcription

17.4.3.1 Standard arrangement

For topical headwords that do not need standardized margin terms, RILM has established a default indexing system that we call standard arrangement. In this system, the first preference in the margin is a person, the second preference is a place, and the third preference is a topic.

Adhering to a default system such as this unifies the index, making it easier to use.

Example 7 presents some standard-arrangement indexing for a topic. Note, for example, that *composers*, being a topic, is only in the margin for an entry that does not indicate a place; in standard arrangement, when a place is indicated (*USA*), it takes precedence over the topic.

Ex. 7: Indexing for women's studies

women's studies
Adorno, T.W.
Australia
    Aboriginal peoples
    music industry
composers
    reception
    19th century
Germany
    cultural policies
    rock musicians
iconography
Mozart, W.A.
    Così fan tutte
        misogynist themes
    Don Giovanni
        character of Donna Elvira
musicians
    blues
    orchestral
popular music
    state of research
    1940s–50s
Queen Latifah
    Ladies first
USA
    ballads
    composers
    musicians
Wagner, R.
    operas
        maternal characters
        women as redeemers

17.5 Enriching your index

During the process of indexing, you may find that new headwords seem appropriate. For example, the presence of entries about operas in example 7 indicates that **opera** would be a useful headword in the same index:

opera
  Mozart, W.A.
    Così fan tutte
      misogynist themes
    Don Giovanni
      character of Donna Elvira
  Wagner, R.
    maternal characters
    women as redeemers

The presence of entries about popular music indicates that the headword **popular music** would be helpful:

popular music
  Germany
    rock
      women musicians
  Queen Latifah
    Ladies first
  women's studies
    state of research
    1940s–50s

Often it makes sense to rotate index levels; for example, the above entries under **popular music** suggest that listings under **Owens, Dana (Queen Latifah)** and **Germany** would be appropriate and helpful. Regrouping entries this way enriches your index, providing many points of access to the information in your book.

Index